JAMESTOWN  EDU

M000190426

English, Yes!

Learning English Through Literature

Level 2: Introductory

 **Glencoe**

New York, New York   Columbus, Ohio   Chicago, Illinois   Peoria, Illinois   Woodland Hills, California

JAMESTOWN EDUCATION

Acknowledgment:
"The Cow, the Mare, and the Sow" by Jane Yolen.
Copyright © 1983 by Jane Yolen. First appeared in *Tales of Wonder,*
published by Schocken Books. Reprinted by permission of Curtis
Brown, Ltd.

Cover photo illustration: Third Eye Image/Solus Photography/Veer.

The *McGraw-Hill* Companies

Send all inquiries to:
Glencoe/McGraw-Hill
8787 Orion Place
Columbus, OH 43240-4027

ISBN 0-07-831109-8
Printed in the United States of America.
1 2 3 4 5 6 7 8 9 10 021 08 07 06 05 04 03

Contents

English, Yes!

Learning English Through Literature

Level 2: Introductory

WHY THE MONSOON COMES EVERY YEAR

This story tells about a very strong storm. The story tells why this bad storm happens.

How do you feel when the weather is bad?

Were you ever in a strong storm?

Why the Monsoon Comes Every Year

a Vietnamese folktale

Long ago in Vietnam there was a great **emperor.** He had a
beautiful and **wise** daughter. His daughter was a princess.
One day the emperor said, "I want the very best husband for
my daughter. I'm looking for a good and **powerful** king."

5 Two kings **heard of** the emperor's search. One was the King of
the Mountains. The other was the King of the Waters. They
both went to the **palace** where the emperor lived.

Which king would be a better husband for the princess? The
emperor had to decide. He gave them both a test. "Come here
10 tomorrow. Bring a special gift for my daughter."

The next morning the King of the Mountains returned. He gave
a box to the princess. A beautiful green stone was in the box.
The stone was jade. The jade came from deep in the king's
mountains. The king said, "This jade has a **perfect** beauty. It is
15 like your beauty." He put his hand on his heart. "But here is my
greatest gift. It is my heart."

The emperor's daughter was happy with the gifts. The emperor was happy too. The sun went down. Still the King of the Waters did not arrive. The princess married the King of the Mountains.
20 They left for the mountains.

During this time, the King of the Waters was **busy.** He was looking for special gifts. He found **precious** coral in the sea. He found lovely pearls. At last he went back to the palace with his gifts. But it was too late. The princess was gone.

25 The King of the Waters was angry. He said, "I'll fight the mountains!" Then he started a great storm. Water came up from the sea. It **pounded** against the land. But the storm could not **destroy** the mountains.

Every year the King of the Waters sends storms to Vietnam.
30 He is thinking about the beautiful princess he lost.

YOU CAN ANSWER THESE QUESTIONS

Put an *x* in the box next to the correct answer.

Reading Comprehension

1. The emperor's daughter was
   - ❑ a. good and powerful.
   - ❑ b. wise and beautiful.

2. The two kings wanted to
   - ❑ a. marry the emperor's daughter.
   - ❑ b. rule the emperor's land.

3. The emperor gave the kings a test. He said,
   - ❑ a. "Bring a special gift for my daughter."
   - ❑ b. "Write a special poem for my daughter."

4. The King of the Mountains gave the daughter
   - ❑ a. precious coral.
   - ❑ b. a beautiful stone and his heart.

5. The King of the Waters
   - ❑ a. didn't bring any gifts.
   - ❑ b. arrived late.

6. The King of the Waters was angry, so he
   - ❑ a. started a big storm.
   - ❑ b. called his soldiers.

7. Every year, the King of the Waters remembers the princess, so he sends
   - ❑ a. storms to Vietnam.
   - ❑ b. a gift to the princess.

Vocabulary

8. The storm did not destroy the mountains. *Destroy* means
   - ❑ a. tear down.
   - ❑ b. spray with water.

9. The water pounded the land. *Pound* means
   - ❑ a. make a lot of noise.
   - ❑ b. hit very hard.

Idioms

10. The kings heard of the emperor's search. *Heard of* means
    - ❑ a. forgot.
    - ❑ b. learned of.

How many questions did you answer correctly? Circle your score. Then fill in your score on the Score Chart on page 152.

Number Correct	1	2	3	4	5	6	7	8	9	10
Score	10	20	30	40	50	60	70	80	90	100

Exercises to help you

Exercise A
Building sentences. Make sentences by adding the correct letter. The first one has been done for you.

1. The emperor wanted ___*b*___

2. Two kings wanted to _____

3. The emperor _____

4. The emperor asked each king _____

  a. marry the princess.
  b. a good husband for his daughter.
  c. gave the two kings a test.
  d. for a special gift for his daughter.

Now write sentences on the lines below. Begin each sentence with a capital letter. End it with a period.

1. _____

2. _____

3. _____

4. _____

Do numbers 5–8 the same way.

5. The King of the Mountains _____

6. The princess left for _____

7. The King of the Waters brought _____

8. The King of the Waters always remembers _____

  a. gifts from the sea.
  b. her new home in the mountains.
  c. gave the princess his heart.
  d. the princess that he lost.

5. _____

6. _____

7. _____

8. _____

Exercise B

Understanding the story. Answer each question. Finish the
sentence. Look back at the line numbers in the story. End each
sentence with a period. The first one has been done for you.

1. Where did the emperor live?

   The emperor lived in Vietnam.

   _____

2. What did the emperor say he wanted?

   The emperor said, "I want the very best husband for my

   _____." line 4

3. Who were the two kings who heard about the
   emperor's daughter?

   The two kings were the King of the Mountains and

   the King of _____ line 6

4. Which king did the princess marry?

   The princess married the King of _____

   _____ line 19

5. What did the King of the Mountains give the princess?

   He gave her jade and his _____

   _____ line 16

6. What does the King of the Waters do every year?

   Every year he sends _____

   _____ line 29

Using subject pronouns correctly. Pronouns are words used in place of nouns. Study the chart.

Subject Pronouns	
Singular	**Plural**
I	we
you	you
he	they
she	
it	

Fill in the blanks. Use the correct subject pronouns. Choose the pronouns from the chart. The first one has been done for you.

1. The emperor said, "I have a beautiful daughter. ____*I*____ want a good husband for my daughter."

2. The princess was very wise. _____ was also very beautiful.

3. The King of the Mountains and the King of the Waters were rulers. _____ were powerful.

4. The King of the Mountains gave two gifts. _____ gave jade—and his heart—to the princess.

5. The princess married the King of the Mountains. _____ left for their home in the mountains.

6. Then the King of the Waters arrived. By then _____ was too late.

Exercise D

Using the present tense of the verb *to be*. Study the chart
below. It shows the present tense of the verb *to be*.

The Verb *to Be:* Present tense	
Singular	**Plural**
I am	we are
you are	you are
he is she is it is	they are

Read the sentences below. Fill in each blank. Use the present
tense of the verb *to be*. The first one has been done for you.

1. The emperor said, "I have a beautiful daughter. She
   _____*is*_____ wise too."

2. The two kings said, "We _____ powerful rulers."

3. The King of the Mountains said to the princess, "You have a
   perfect beauty. You _____ like the jade."

4. The emperor and the princess said, "We like the gifts. They
   _____ special."

5. The emperor said, "The King of the Waters is not here. He
   _____ late."

6. The King of the Waters said, "I _____ angry."

Exercise E

Working with adjectives. Study the chart.

An adjective is a word that tells something about a noun.

Example:　　The emperor lived in a *big* palace.

An adjective usually comes before a noun.
It also can come after the verb *to be*.

　　　　　　　　　　　　　　　　　　　　　　noun
Examples:　　The emperor had a *beautiful* daughter.

　　　　　　　　verb—*to be*
　　　　　　　The daughter <u>was</u> *beautiful*.

Complete the sentences below. Use adjectives from the box.
Use each adjective once. The first one has been done for you.

powerful	precious	special	wise

1. The princess was beautiful and *wise* .

2. Two _____ kings wanted to marry the princess.

3. The emperor said, "Bring my daughter a _____ gift."

4. The King of the Waters found _____ coral. The coral was difficult to find.

Exercise F

Putting the words in order. Write sentences with the words given. Put the words in the correct order. All the sentences have adjectives. The first one has been done for you.

1. got / a / gift / The princess / special

    The princess got a special gift.

2. jade / was / The / perfect

    _____

3. found / pearls / lovely / One king

    _____

Exercise G
Speaking up. Look at the conversation. Practice with two other students.

SHARING WITH OTHERS

Activity A
Understanding characters. Work in a small group. Read the list of characters below. Then write three or four sentences that each character might say. Use a separate piece of paper for each character.

- the emperor
- the princess
- the King of the Mountains
- the King of the Waters

Example:
I heard about a beautiful princess. I wanted to marry the princess. I gave a special gift. I gave my heart.

Exchange your papers with another group. Can they guess who the characters are?

Activity B
Sharing ideas. Everyone can learn by sharing ideas. Discuss these questions with your partner or with the group. Write your answer to one of the questions.

The princess married the King of the Mountains. Was he the best husband for the princess? Why or why not?

This folktale tells why there are monsoons in Vietnam every year. Do you know a story about how something in nature began? What is the story about? Who are the characters?

Who is your favorite character in the story? Why?

A LESSON FROM
TWO LITTLE GIRLS

This story tells about two friends.
What things do you do with your friends for fun?
Do you like to talk together?
Do you sometimes argue? How do the arguments end?

A Lesson from Two Little Girls

based on a story by Leo Tolstoy

It was early spring. The snow was melting. Water ran in **streams** down the village street.

Two little girls began to play in the street. Malasha was the younger girl. She was wearing her new blue dress. Akoulya was the older girl. She was wearing her new yellow dress. The girls decided to play in a big **puddle.**

Akoulya **warned,** "We can't get our new clothes dirty. Our mothers will be angry." So they **took off** their shoes. Then they raised their skirts just a little. This would keep the skirts dry.

Akoulya said, "Don't **splash.** Walk carefully."

Just then, Malasha put her foot down hard in the puddle. Water splashed onto Akoulya's dress. It even splashed on her face.

Akoulya was angry. She ran after Malasha. Just then Akoulya's mother was passing by. She saw her daughter's dirty dress.

"Akoulya! What did you do to your new dress?"

"Malasha splashed me. She did it **on purpose,**" said Akoulya.

Akoulya's mother turned to Malasha. "Why did you do this?" she asked in a loud voice. Malasha began to cry.

Malasha's mother heard her daughter. She ran out of her house.

20 The two mothers began **arguing.** A crowd gathered. Soon
everyone was **shouting** and arguing.

During this time, Akoulya went back to the puddle. She started
to play. Malasha joined her. They put a piece of wood into the
puddle. It quickly moved into a stream. It floated down the
25 street. The girls ran after it.

They shouted, "Catch it! Catch it!"

The girls ran right into the crowd. The people were still arguing.

An older woman called out, "People, aren't you **ashamed?** You
are fighting. But the girls don't **remember** their fight. They are
30 playing together. The girls are wiser than you are."

The people looked at each other. It was true. The girls were not
fighting. The people felt a little ashamed. They remembered now
that they were friends and neighbors. They had learned a lesson
from the two little girls.

YOU CAN ANSWER THESE QUESTIONS

Put an *x* in the box next to the correct answer.

Reading Comprehension

1. The girls wanted to play
   - ❏ a. in a puddle on the street.
   - ❏ b. near the river by their homes.

2. Malasha put her foot down hard, and
   - ❏ a. Malasha's dress got a lot of water on it.
   - ❏ b. water splashed on Akoulya's face and dress.

3. Akoulya told her mother that
   - ❏ a. Malasha splashed her.
   - ❏ b. she fell into the puddle.

4. Akoulya's mother and Malasha's mother
   - ❏ a. told their daughters to go home.
   - ❏ b. began to argue.

5. Soon everyone
   - ❏ a. wanted to see the puddle.
   - ❏ b. began arguing in the street.

6. The two girls began to
   - ❏ a. play again.
   - ❏ b. fight again.

7. The people learned
   - ❏ a. not to argue about things that are not important.
   - ❏ b. that only children should fight.

Vocabulary

8. The two mothers argued in the street. *Argue* means
   - ❏ a. to fight, using words.
   - ❏ b. to try to understand.

9. At the end, the people were ashamed. *Ashamed* means
   - ❏ a. feeling bad because you did something wrong.
   - ❏ b. feeling scared.

Idioms

10. Akoulya said that Malasha had splashed her on purpose. *On purpose* means
   - ❏ a. by mistake, without trying to.
   - ❏ b. by trying to.

How many questions did you answer correctly? Circle your score. Then fill in your score on the Score Chart on page 152.

Number Correct	1	2	3	4	5	6	7	8	9	10
Score	10	20	30	40	50	60	70	80	90	100

EXERCISES TO HELP YOU

Exercise A

Building sentences. Make sentences by adding the correct letter.

1. The little girls began ___*c*___

2. Their dresses were _____

3. One girl _____

4. The mother saw _____

    a. new.
    b. splashed the other girl.
    c. to play in the street.
    d. her daughter's dirty dress.

Now write the sentences on the lines below. Begin each sentence with a capital letter. End it with a period.

1. _____

2. _____

3. _____

4. _____

Do numbers 5–8 the same way.

5. Malasha's mother _____

6. The mothers were _____

7. The girls started to _____

8. The older people learned _____

    a. arguing.
    b. a lesson.
    c. play again.
    d. ran out of her house.

5. _____

6. _____

7. _____

8. _____

Understanding the story. Answer each question. Finish each sentence. Look back at the line numbers in the story. End each sentence with a period. The first one has been done for you.

1. Where did the little girls begin to play?

    They began to play in the street.

    _____

2. Which girl's dress did water splash onto?

    Water splashed onto _____

    dress. _____ line 12

3. What did Akoulya's mother do?

    She asked Malasha, "Why did _____

    _____ line 17

4. Soon what was everyone doing?

    Soon everyone was shouting and _____

    _____ line 21

5. What did the older woman call out?

    She called out, "People, aren't you _____

    _____ line 28

6. What did the people learn?

    The people learned a _____

    _____ line 33

Using possessive pronouns correctly. Possessive pronouns show who owns something. Study this chart. It shows possessive pronouns that describe nouns.

Possessive Pronouns	
Singular	**Plural**
my	our
your	your
his	their
her	
its	

Fill in the blanks. Use the correct possessive pronouns. The first one has been done for you.

1. Malasha had a good friend. ___*Her*___ friend was Akoulya.

2. They were wearing dresses. _____ dresses were new.

3. Akoulya said to Malasha, "_____ mothers want us to keep the dresses clean."

4. Akoulya warned Malasha, "Don't get _____ dress dirty."

5. The people were shouting. _____ voices were loud.

6. An older woman said, "The girls are wiser than you are." The people listened to _____ words.

Using past-tense verbs correctly. Regular past-tense verbs end in *ed*. Study this chart.

Regular Past-Tense Verbs
shout + **ed** = shouted
look + **ed** = looked
like + **d** = liked
decide + **d** = decided

Fill in the blanks with verbs in the past tense. Use the verbs under the lines. The first one has been done for you.

1. The little girls ___*wanted*___ to play in the puddle.
   want

2. The children _____ their skirts just a little to keep
   raise
   them dry.

3. Water _____ on Akoulya's dress.
   splash

4. The two mothers _____ and argued.
   shout

5. People _____ around the women.
   gather

6. The piece of wood _____ down the street.
   float

Exercise E

Understanding vocabulary. Read the words in the box. These words are from the story. Write each word in the correct place in the chart. Some have been done for you.

blue	dress	face	foot	skirt	shoes	yellow

Parts of the Body	Colors	Clothes
face	blue	dress

Understanding opposites. Opposites are words with completely different meanings. For example, *little* is the opposite of *big*. Complete the crossword puzzle below.

Look at each clue at the bottom of the page. Find the opposite in the box. Write that word in the puzzle. The first one has been done for you.

fall	late	little	old	catch	remember	loud	dirty

Opposites

Across
1. spring
4. young
6. forget

Down
2. drop
3. quiet
5. clean
7. early
8. big

Speaking up. Look at the conversation and then practice with a partner.

SHARING WITH OTHERS

Activity A

Acting out the story. Work in a group. Pretend to be one of these characters:

- Akoulya
- Malasha
- Akoulya's mother
- Malasha's mother
- The older woman
- Someone in the crowd

Use sentences from the story. Add your own words. Present your play to the class.

Activity B

Sharing ideas. Everyone can learn by sharing ideas. Which of the following ideas do you think best explains the lesson of the story? Share your opinion with a partner or a group.

People sometimes fight over things that are not important.

It is best to stay friends with other people.

People should forgive friends who make mistakes.

Children don't stay angry, but adults often stay angry.

HOW THE PEOPLE BECAME WISE

Think of someone who is wise.

Why do you think the person is wise?

How does a person become wise?

How the People Became Wise

a West African folktale

There once was a man named Father Anansi. Father Anansi lived among the Fanti people of West Africa. He had all of the wisdom in the world. People came to him every day for **advice** and help.

5 One day the people made Father Anansi angry. He decided to **punish** them. He thought and thought about what he would do.

Father Anansi decided to hide all of his wisdom. He took back all of his wisdom from the people. He put the wisdom into a large pot. The next morning he quietly left his house. The pot
10 of wisdom was hanging from his neck.

Father Anansi had a son. The son's name was Kweku Tsin. The son knew that his father was very angry. He watched his father closely. Kweku Tsin followed his father that morning. Father Anansi did not see his son.

15 Father Anansi walked very far into the forest. He stopped under a tall tree. There were many plants around the tree. It was not easy to get close to the tree. With much **effort,** Father Anansi reached the tree. He started to **climb.**

Father Anansi wanted to hang the pot of wisdom from the top
of the tree. "Then no one will get any wisdom," he thought.
"People won't be able to climb this tall tree."

It was hard even for Father Anansi to climb the tree. He had
the **heavy** pot in front of him. Again and again he tried to get to
the top of the tree. Again and again he **failed.**

Kweku Tsin watched his father for a long time. The son saw
that his father was climbing in the wrong way. Father Anansi
was climbing with the pot in front of him. **Finally,** the son
jumped up. He said **loudly,** "Father, **why don't you** hang the pot
on your back? Then you can climb to the top more quickly."

Father Anansi looked at his son. "I thought I had all of the wisdom in the world in this pot," Father Anansi said. "You have
more wisdom than I have. All of the wisdom in this pot did not
show me what to do." Father Anansi was very angry. He threw
the pot down. It hit a large rock and broke open. The wisdom
escaped. It **spread** to all of the people.

Put an *x* in the box next to the correct answer.

Reading Comprehension

1. People went to Father Anansi for
   - ❏ a. money.
   - ❏ b. advice.

2. At the start of the story, Father Anansi became
   - ❏ a. angry.
   - ❏ b. sick.

3. Father Anansi's plan was to
   - ❏ a. hide his wisdom.
   - ❏ b. give wisdom to his son.

4. It was hard for Father Anansi to climb the tree because
   - ❏ a. the tree's branches were thick.
   - ❏ b. he was carrying a heavy pot in front of him.

5. The son told his father to
   - ❏ a. give the wisdom back to the people.
   - ❏ b. put the pot on his back.

6. Father Anansi threw the pot down because he was
   - ❏ a. angry that his son had wisdom.
   - ❏ b. tired from climbing.

7. At the end of the story, wisdom went
   - ❏ a. to the people.
   - ❏ b. on top of the tree.

Vocabulary

8. Father Anansi wanted to punish the people because he was angry. The word *punish* means
   - ❏ a. to hide something from someone.
   - ❏ b. to make life difficult for someone because the person did something wrong.

9. Father Anansi reached the tree after much effort. The word *effort* means
   - ❏ a. trying.
   - ❏ b. talking.

Idioms

10. The son said, "Father, why don't you hang the pot on your back?" The idiom *why don't you* means
    - ❏ a. "You should try doing this."
    - ❏ b. "I don't understand what you are doing."

How many questions did you answer correctly? Circle your score. Then fill in your score on the Score Chart on page 152.

Number Correct	1	2	3	4	5	6	7	8	9	10
Score	10	20	30	40	50	60	70	80	90	100

EXERCISES TO HELP YOU

Exercise A

Building sentences. Make sentences by adding the correct letter. The first one has been done for you.

1. Father Anansi had _____ *c* _____   **a.** into a pot.

                                           b. angry with the people.

2. He became _____   **c.** all of the world's wisdom.

                                           d. hide his wisdom.

3. He decided to _____

4. He put the wisdom _____

Now write the sentences on the lines below. Begin each sentence with a capital letter. End it with a period.

1. _____

2. _____

3. _____

4. _____

Do numbers 5–8 the same way.

5. The son followed _____   **a.** a tree with the pot in front of him.

6. Father Anansi climbed _____   **b.** Father Anansi into the forest.

7. The son told him to _____   **c.** angry and threw the pot down.

8. Father Anansi was _____   **d.** put the pot on his back.

5. _____

6. _____

7. _____

8. _____

Exercise B

Understanding the story. Answer each question. Finish each sentence. Look back at the line numbers in the story. End each sentence with a period. The first one has been done for you.

1. Where did Father Anansi live?

Father Anansi lived among the Fanti people

of West Africa.

2. What did Father Anansi decide to do to the people?

He decided to

them. _____ line 6

3. What did Father Anansi decide to hide?

He decided to hide all of his

_____ line 7

4. What was the name of Father Anansi's son?

The son's name was

_____ line 11

5. Why was it difficult for Father Anansi to climb the tree?

Father Anansi had a

in front of him. _____ line 23

6. What happened to the wisdom at the end of the story?

The wisdom spread

_____ line 35

Studying irregular past-tense verbs. Some verbs in the past tense do not end in *ed*. These verbs are called irregular verbs.

Here are some irregular verbs. The verbs are in the present tense. Look at the story. Find the past tense of each verb. Complete the verb. The first one has been done for you.

1. has   *h a* d   7. leaves   _ _ f _

2. comes   _ a _ _   8. knows   _ _ _ w

3. makes   _ _ _ e   9. says   _ _ i _

4. thinks   _ _ o u _ _ _   10. throws   _ h _ _ _

5. takes   _ _ o _   11. hits   _ _ t

6. puts   _ u _   12. spreads   _ _ _ e a _

Exercise D
Using past-tense verbs. Write each sentence or question. Change the underlined verb to past tense. The first one has been done for you.

1. Father Anansi <u>has</u> wisdom.

   Father Anansi had wisdom.

2. Who <u>makes</u> Father Anansi angry?

   _____

3. He <u>thinks</u> about what to do with his wisdom.

   _____

4. He <u>puts</u> all of the wisdom into a pot.

   _____

5. He <u>takes</u> the pot to a tall tree.

   _____

6. His son <u>says</u>, "Father, why don't you hang the pot on your back?"

   _____

Exercise E

Using prepositions correctly. Study the chart.

A preposition joins words in a sentence. It often shows position or direction.
Examples: People came *to* him every day.   He took back all *of* his wisdom.   He put the wisdom *into* a large pot.

Fill in the blanks by adding the correct preposition from the box. Each sentence says something about the story. Use each preposition once. The first one has been done for you.

at   for   from   of   into   to

1. People went ____*to*____ Father Anansi.

2. People went _____ advice.

3. Father Anansi took back his wisdom _____ the people.

4. He walked far _____ the forest.

5. He stopped _____ a tall tree.

6. The pot _____ wisdom broke.

Write your own sentences about the story. Use the groups of words below in your sentences. Begin each sentence with a capital letter. End it with a period.

7. went to

_____

8. went for

_____

9. walked into

_____

10. around his neck

_____

11. At the end of the story

_____

Understanding vocabulary. Knowing action verbs will help you to understand stories. Match the verbs from the story with their meanings. Write the correct letter in the blank. The first one has been done for you.

1. climbed ___*a*___   **a.** went up

2. escaped _____   **b.** moved behind someone

3. failed _____   **c.** was not able to do something

4. followed _____   **d.** became free; got out of

5. reached _____   **e.** moved to all parts of an area

6. spread _____   **f.** came to; arrived at

Exercise G

Using vocabulary. Complete the sentences. They tell something about the story. Use the verbs in Exercise F. Use each verb once. The first one has been done for you.

1. The son _*followed*_ Father Anansi into the forest.

2. There were many plants around a tall tree. With much effort, Father Anansi finally _____ the tree.

3. Father Anansi _____ up the tall tree.

4. He _____ to get to the top of the tree.

5. The pot of wisdom broke. Wisdom _____ from the pot.

6. Wisdom _____ to all of the people.

Exercise H

Speaking up. Look at the conversation. Practice it with a partner.

SHARING WITH OTHERS

Activity A
Retelling the story. Tell the story as if you were Father Anansi, the son, or one of the Fanti people.

Example:
The son
My father is the famous Father Anansi. People go to him for advice. One day he was angry at the people. I knew he was angry. I knew he wanted to punish the people. I watched him. One morning he went into the forest. I followed him.

Activity B
Sharing ideas. Everyone can learn by sharing ideas. Discuss these questions with your partner or with the group. Write your answer to one of the questions.

What words describe Father Anansi?
very wise   very understanding
quick to get angry   always right

What words describe the son?
smart   understanding of other people
kind to his father   always right

Do you think Father Anansi is wise? Why or why not?

Suppose you had a problem. Would you go to Father Anansi for advice? Why or why not?

Activity C
Extending the story. This tale tells how people became wise. It is good to be wise. Here are some other good ways to be. Look up the words in a dictionary. Discuss their meanings.

calm   generous   cheerful   understanding   smart

Imagine that you can choose one of these words and have all people be that way. Which one do you choose? Why? Write your answer. Discuss your answer with others.

THE ENVELOPE

Do you like to hear scary stories or go to scary movies?
Do you like to tell scary stories?
Think about some ghost stories you know.

The Envelope

an urban legend

A married couple was traveling in the country. The husband and wife were **on the way** to the home of friends in another state. The weather was bad. It was rainy. Soon it got dark. The couple wanted to find a place to sleep. They started to look for a **motel.**

5   The travelers lost their way. Everything around them was dark. There were tall trees on both sides of the road. Then suddenly they saw a light. It was in the window of a house. The couple drove down a short road to the house. They rang the doorbell.

An older man and woman came to the door. They were
10   surprised to see travelers. But they welcomed the couple.

The travelers said that they would like to stay for the night. They **offered** to pay for a room. The older man **refused.** He said, "You can stay, but we don't want any money. You are our guests."

15   So the two couples ate supper together. They **chatted** at the dinner table. The two men were talking. The younger man again offered to pay. He said, "We want to leave very **early** in the morning. Can we give you some money now?" The older man again refused to take the money.

20   Then both couples went to sleep. The next morning the younger couple left very early. The wife put some money in an envelope. She left the envelope on a table near the door.

The couple **drove off.** They stopped for breakfast in a small restaurant in the next **town.** It wasn't far away. They started
25   to talk to the restaurant owner about the older couple. The husband explained, "Those people were very nice to us. Do you know who they are?" The owner said, "Tell me more about the couple and the house." The younger couple told him more. The man looked surprised. "I know the house and the people. They
30   were the Norths. But there was a fire at their house three years ago. Their house was **ruined.** Both of them died in the fire."

There was an argument between the couple and the owner. The couple asked the owner to go back to the house with them. All three drove back to the Norths' house. In fact, there was no
35   house. There were just some **burned** walls with no roof. The wife looked inside. She saw a burned table. She screamed. On the table was her envelope.

YOU CAN ANSWER THESE QUESTIONS

Put an *x* in the box next to the correct answer.

Reading Comprehension

1. It was getting dark, and the couple wanted a place
   - ❏ a. to eat.
   - ❏ b. to sleep.

2. The couple found
   - ❏ a. a motel in the country.
   - ❏ b. a house where an older couple lived.

3. The older couple refused
   - ❏ a. to let the younger couple spend the night.
   - ❏ b. to take money.

4. The next day, the wife
   - ❏ a. left money in an envelope.
   - ❏ b. forgot something at the house.

5. The restaurant owner said that
   - ❏ a. he didn't know of the house.
   - ❏ b. the house had burned down.

6. The wife found the envelope
   - ❏ a. in the burned house.
   - ❏ b. in the car.

7. The older couple had
   - ❏ a. lived in the house but had died.
   - ❏ b. never lived in the house.

Vocabulary

8. The couples ate and chatted at the dinner table. The word *chat* means
   - ❏ a. talk.
   - ❏ b. eat a lot.

9. The older man refused to take money for the room. The word *refuse* means
   - ❏ a. say no to something.
   - ❏ b. not understand something.

Idioms

10. The couple was on the way to the house of friends. The idiom *on the way* means
    - ❏ a. wanting something of one's own.
    - ❏ b. going from one place to another.

How many questions did you answer correctly? Circle your score. Then fill in your score on the Score Chart on page 152.

Number Correct	1	2	3	4	5	6	7	8	9	10
Score	10	20	30	40	50	60	70	80	90	100

Exercise A

Building sentences. Make sentences by adding the correct
letter. The first one has been done for you.

1. The younger couple
   wanted to stop _____*b*_____

2. The older couple _____

3. The younger couple
   wanted to _____

4. The older man refused _____

   a. welcomed the younger
      couple.
   b. for the night.
   c. to take money.
   d. pay for the room.

Now write the sentences on the lines below. Begin each
sentence with a capital letter. End it with a period.

1. _____

2. _____

3. _____

4. _____

Now do numbers 5–8 the same way.

5. The younger couple _____

6. They talked to _____

7. They drove back to
   the house _____

8. There was _____

   a. an envelope on a burned
      table.
   b. with the restaurant owner.
   c. left early the next
      morning.
   d. the restaurant owner.

5. _____

6. _____

7. _____

8. _____

Understanding the story. Answer each question. Finish each
sentence. Look back at the line numbers in the story. End each
sentence with a period. The first one has been done for you.

1. How was the weather during the couple's trip?

    The weather was rainy.

    _____

2. Where did the travelers see a light?

    They saw a light in the _____

    _____ line 7

3. Who came to the door?

    An older man and _____

    came to the door. _____ line 9

4. What did the husband and wife want to pay for?

    They wanted to pay for _____

    _____ line 12

5. Where did the couple and restaurant owner drive?

    They drove back _____

    _____ line 34

6. What did they see there?

    They saw _____

    _____ line 35

Exercise C

Using plural nouns. Some nouns in English are used for one person or thing. They are called singular nouns. When the nouns are used for two or more persons or things, they are called plural nouns.

Most plural nouns end in *s*.

Singular	Plural
(one) house	(three) houses
(one) envelope	(two) envelopes

Other plural nouns do not end in *s*. They are irregular.

Singular	Plural
man	men
woman	women
deer	deer

Complete each sentence. Write the plural form of the noun that is under the line. The first one has been done for you.

1. There were two *travelers* in the car.
   traveler

2. There were many _____ on the sides of the road.
   tree

3. Some _____ stood beside the road.
   deer

4. The two married _____ had dinner together.
   couple

5. The two _____ talked about money.
   man

6. The two _____ were also at the dinner table.
   woman

Using the verbs *was* and *were* correctly. Study this chart.

The Verb *to Be:* Past Tense	
Singular	**Plural**
I was	we were
you were	you were
he was	they were
she was	
it was	

Fill in each blank. Use the past tense of the verb *to be*. The first one has been done for you.

1. The travelers ___*were*___ on their way to the house of friends.

2. It _____ rainy and dark.

3. They told the restaurant owner, "We _____ surprised to see a light in a window."

4. They said, "A man came to the door. He _____ nice."

5. The restaurant owner said, "I _____ a friend of Mr. and Mrs. North."

6. The envelope _____ on the table.

Exercise E

Using *there was* and *there were* correctly. Study the chart. Use *there was* before singular nouns. Use *there were* before plural nouns.

There was a <u>car</u> in the street.
There were many <u>cars</u> on the street.

Fill in each blank. Use *there was* or *there were*. The first one has been done for you.

1. _There were_____ two people in the car.

2. _____ a light in the window.

3. _____ a man and a woman at the door.

4. _____ a restaurant in town.

5. _____ just some burned walls.

6. _____ an envelope on the table.

Exercise F

Understanding vocabulary. Match the words from the story with their meanings. Write the correct letter in the blank. The first one has been done for you.

1. ruined ___*f*___

2. burned _____

3. early _____

4. motel _____

5. offer _____

6. town _____

a. before the usual time
b. a place that rents rooms for sleeping
c. to try to give
d. a small city
e. touched by fire
f. broken and destroyed

Speaking up. Look at the conversations. Practice them with a partner.

SHARING WITH OTHERS

Activity A

Putting the story in order. Do this activity.

1. Choose five sentences from different parts of the story.
2. Write each sentence on a separate piece of paper.
3. Work with a partner. Give your partner your sentences. Take your partner's sentences.
4. Put the sentences you have in order. Put the sentence that came first in the story. Put the sentence that came second in the story next. Continue in this way.
5. Check your partner's work. Are the sentences in the correct order?

Activity B

Sharing ideas. Everyone can learn by sharing ideas. Discuss these questions with your partner or with the group. Write your answer to three of the questions.

When and where does the story take place?
What is the problem for the two main characters?
What is the solution?

Where are the main characters at the end of the story?
What is the surprise at the end?
What makes the ending scary?

THE SMELL OF FOOD
AND THE SOUND OF COINS

Think about a person you talk to when you have a problem.
Does that person give good ideas about what to do?
Do people ever come to you for advice?
Is it easy or hard to give advice? Why?

The Smell of Food and the Sound of Coins

a folktale from Central Asia

Long ago, in Asia, there was a famous judge. People **respected** her. She **made** good **decisions.** She knew the law, and she helped the poor.

One day, a poor traveler was in the market of the town. He sat
5   near a food **stand.** The owner of the stand was cooking fish.

The traveler ate his own rice and vegetables. The fish smelled good. The traveler ate his food, and he enjoyed the smell of the fish. He ate slowly. He thought of the **tasty** fish.

Suddenly the owner of the stand came up to the traveler. "You
10 have to pay me for the smell of my fish." The traveler **replied,** "But I didn't eat anything. So I don't have to pay you."

The **pair** started to argue in the market. Soon a crowd gathered. A person in the crowd said, "This is a difficult problem. Go to our judge."

15 So the traveler and the stand owner went to the judge.

The owner said, "This man sat near my stand for half an hour.

He ate his rice and vegetables. He enjoyed the smell of my fish while he ate his food. He has to give me something for that."

The judge thought for **a while.** Then she said, "That sounds fair. Traveler, you have to give him something for the smell of his food. You enjoyed the smell. Do you **agree?**"

The traveler replied, "I stopped in the market. I wanted to buy a meal. But the food cost too much. I have only **a few coins** for my trip. So I ate my own rice. I ate my own vegetables. I didn't eat the man's food. So I don't have to pay him any money."

The judge said, "You have a few coins. Please give them to me." The traveler was not happy, but he gave the coins to the judge.

The judge closed her hands around the coins. She slowly **shook** the coins. They made a **jingling** sound. Then she gave the coins back to the traveler.

The owner was angry. "Why did you give the coins back?"

The judge replied, "It is only fair. The traveler smelled your fish. But he didn't eat any. You heard the sound of his coins. But you don't get any. You see, he pays for the smell of your fish with the sound of his coins."

YOU CAN ANSWER THESE QUESTIONS

Put an *x* in the box next to the correct answer.

Reading Comprehension

1. The poor traveler ate
   - ❏ a. his own fish.
   - ❏ b. his own rice and vegetables.

2. The stand owner wanted the traveler to
   - ❏ a. share his food.
   - ❏ b. give him something.

3. The stand owner said that the traveler
   - ❏ a. enjoyed the smell of his fish.
   - ❏ b. took a fish.

4. The traveler
   - ❏ a. wanted to pay the stand owner.
   - ❏ b. did not want to pay the stand owner.

5. The judge shook the coins, and then she
   - ❏ a. gave them back to the traveler.
   - ❏ b. gave them to the stand owner.

6. The judge said that the stand owner
   - ❏ a. enjoyed the smell of the food.
   - ❏ b. heard the sound of the coins.

Vocabulary

7. People respected the judge. When you *respect* someone, you think that the person is
   - ❏ a. good or wise.
   - ❏ b. very busy.

8. The judge was fair. She listened to both sides of a story. Being *fair* means
   - ❏ a. treating different people the same way.
   - ❏ b. choosing the person you like best.

Idioms

9. The judge made good decisions. To *make a decision* means to
   - ❏ a. think about a problem.
   - ❏ b. pick an answer to a problem.

10. The traveler said that he had only a few coins. *A few* means
    - ❏ a. many.
    - ❏ b. not many.

How many questions did you answer correctly? Circle your score. Then fill in your score on the Score Chart on page 152.

Number Correct	1	2	3	4	5	6	7	8	9	10
Score	10	20	30	40	50	60	70	80	90	100

EXERCISES TO HELP YOU

Exercise A

Building sentences. Make sentences by adding the correct letter. The first one has been done for you.

1. A poor traveler visited _____*c*_____

2. He ate _____

3. He enjoyed the smell _____

4. The stand's owner asked the traveler _____

a. of fish from a stand.
b. his own food.
c. a town market.
d. to pay him.

Now write the sentences on the lines below. Begin each sentence with a capital letter. End it with a period.

1. _____

2. _____

3. _____

4. _____

Do numbers 5–8 the same way.

5. The traveler didn't want _____

6. The two men _____

7. The judge took _____

8. She gave the coins _____

a. argued in the market.
b. the traveler's coins.
c. to pay the owner.
d. back to the traveler.

5. _____

6. _____

7. _____

8. _____

Understanding the story. Answer each question. Finish each sentence. Look back at the line numbers in the story. End each sentence with a period. The first one has been done for you.

1. Where did the traveler sit?

   He sat near a food stand in the town market.

   _____

2. What did the traveler eat?

   He ate rice and _____

   _____ line 6

3. What did the food stand owner say to the traveler?

   He said, "You have to _____

   for the smell of my fish. _____ line 10

4. What did the traveler reply?

   The traveler said that he didn't _____,

   so he didn't have to pay. _____ line 11

5. What did the judge do with the traveler's coins?

   She closed her hands around the coins. She _____

   _____ lines 28–29

6. To whom did the judge give the coins?

   She gave them back _____

   _____ line 30

Exercise C

Using negatives in the past tense. Negative sentences are sentences that have the word *not* in them. In the past tense, negative sentences often have *did* + *not*. The contraction for *did not* is *didn't*.

Example:
The traveler *didn't eat* fish.

Note that the base form of the verb is used with *didn't* and *did not*. Study the chart.

Past Tense	Negative in the Past Tense
ate	didn't eat (did not eat)
went	didn't go (did not go)
respected	didn't respect (did not respect)

Complete the sentences. Use negative verbs in the past tense. Use the verbs under the lines. Use contractions. The first one has been done for you.

1. The traveler _____ *didn't have* _____ a lot of money.
   <u>have</u>
   He had only a few coins.

2. The traveler _____ fish.
   <u>buy</u>
   He ate his own food.

3. The traveler _____ money to the stand
   <u>give</u>
   owner. He had only smelled the fish.

4. The traveler and the stand owner _____
   <u>agree</u>
   They argued in the street.

5. The people in the market _____ what to
   <u>know</u>
   do. One said, "Go to our judge."

6. At the end of the story, the judge _____
   <u>take</u>
   the side of the stand owner.

Exercise D

Asking questions in the past tense. Questions often contain the words *do* or *does*. In the past tense, questions often use *did*. Study the chart.

Common Form for Questions in the Past Tense
Who, what, when, where, or *why* + *did* + subject + base verb
Examples: What **did** the judge **decide**?   What **did** the traveler **say**?

Read the sentence. Then complete each question in the past tense. Use the word *did* and the base form of the underlined verb. The first one has been done for you.

1. The judge <u>knew</u> the law.

    What ____*did*____ the judge ____*know*____?

2. The traveler <u>ate</u> his own rice and vegetables.

    What _____ the traveler _____?

3. The traveler <u>enjoyed</u> the smell of fish.

    What _____ the traveler _____?

4. The stand owner <u>wanted</u> money.

    What _____ the stand owner _____?

5. The traveler and the stand owner <u>decided</u> to see the judge.

    What _____ the traveler and the stand owner
    _____?

6. The stand owner <u>heard</u> the sound of coins.

    What _____ the stand owner _____?

Understanding vocabulary. Match the words with their meanings. Write the correct letter in the blank. The first one has been done for you.

1. tasty ___*e*___

2. pair _____

3. replied _____

4. coins _____

5. jingling _____

6. agree _____

a. answered
b. ringing lightly
c. think the same thing
d. two people or two things
e. good to eat
f. pieces of money

Exercise F

Using vocabulary. Complete the sentences. They tell about the story. Use the vocabulary words from Exercise E. Use each word once. The first one has been done for you.

1. The traveler didn't have ___*tasty*___ fish to eat. He had just rice and vegetables.

2. The stand owner wanted the traveler to pay. The traveler _____ , "I didn't eat anything."

3. The stand owner and the traveler started to argue. They couldn't _____ .

4. The _____ went before the judge.

5. The judge held the _____ in her hands.

6. She shook them, and they made a _____ sound.

Exercise G

Speaking up. Look at the conversation. Practice it with a partner.

SHARING WITH OTHERS

Activity A

Thinking about the story. Imagine that you are the judge in the story. What decision will you make? Discuss these possible decisions with a partner.

1. The traveler has to buy a fish from the stand. In this way, the owner gets some money, and the traveler gets some fish.
2. The traveler has to pay the stand owner a very small amount of money.
3. The traveler must work all day at the stand. Then he gets a free meal of fish.
4. The stand owner has to give the traveler a free meal. This is because he caused the poor traveler a lot of trouble.

Activity B

Sharing ideas. Everyone can learn by sharing ideas. Discuss these questions with your partner or with the group. Write your answer to one of the questions.

Do you think the judge made a good decision? Why or why not?

Who is your favorite character in the story? Why?

DON QUIXOTE AND THE WINDMILLS

What do you know about knights?

What did knights fight for?

Who is like a knight today? Why?

What good causes do people fight for?

Don Quixote and the Windmills

based on a story by Miguel de Cervantes

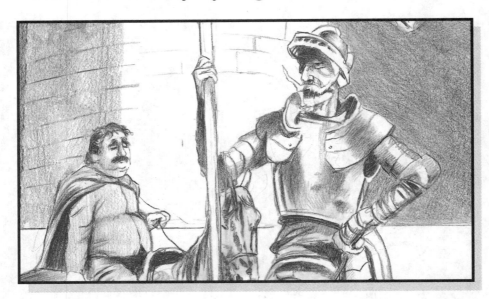

Don Quixote lived in a village in Spain a long time ago. He began to read books about knights. The books told about knights' great **adventures.** Don Quixote sold some of his land, and he bought even more books.

5   Don Quixote spent more and more time reading about knights. He slept less and less. He started to have **strange** ideas. He wasn't a young man, but he decided to become a knight. Don Quixote wanted to ride through the country. He wanted to do good deeds. He wanted to look for adventure.

10   Don Quixote made himself a suit of armor. Then he looked for a helper. He talked to a neighbor named Sancho Panza. Sancho wasn't very smart. Don Quixote made **promises.** He told Sancho that knights get **rewards**. "Knights even **receive** land," said Don Quixote. "If I get an island, I'll give it to you."

15   Sancho agreed to be Don Quixote's helper.

Don Quixote sold many of his things. He needed money for his plan. One day he told Sancho, "It's time to leave." Sancho rode on a donkey. Don Quixote rode on his thin horse. No one in the village saw them leave.

20　The next day the two men saw something in a field ahead. "We have good luck, Sancho!" shouted Don Quixote. "Look, there are some giants with long arms. They are **evil,** and we must fight them!"

"Please look again, sir," Sancho said. "Those are not giants.
25　They are windmills. The arms turn when the wind blows."

"You do not know about adventures!" Don Quixote said. "You are afraid of the giants. I will fight them by myself." Don Quixote pointed his **lance** at a windmill. His horse ran toward it.

The wind began to blow. The arms of the windmills began to
30　turn. Don Quixote's lance went through one of the arms. The arm moved quickly. It knocked Don Quixote off his horse. It broke the lance into pieces.

Sancho went to help Don Quixote. "Sir, these are windmills."

Don Quixote said, "Be quiet, Sancho. Someone used magic. He
35　**turned** the giants **into** windmills. I'll find this person. I will fight him with my **sword.**"

"So be it," Sancho said. Don Quixote got back on his horse. The two men **rode off.** They would look for new adventures.

YOU CAN ANSWER THESE QUESTIONS

Put an *x* in the box next to the correct answer.

Reading Comprehension

1. Don Quixote wasn't
- ❏ a. a young man.
- ❏ b. an older man.

2. Don Quixote read books about
- ❏ a. knights.
- ❏ b. strange ideas.

3. Don Quixote decided to
- ❏ a. become a knight.
- ❏ b. find a knight.

4. Don Quixote got ready. He
- ❏ a. made a suit of armor and got a helper.
- ❏ b. bought a suit and got a job.

5. Don Quixote and Sancho saw windmills. Don Quixote thought that they were
- ❏ a. windmills.
- ❏ b. giants.

6. Don Quixote pointed his lance. He fought. Then he thought that he
- ❏ a. had fought giants who became windmills.
- ❏ b. had fought windmills.

Vocabulary

7. Don Quixote told Sancho that knights get rewards. The word *reward* means
- ❏ a. something you get for doing something good.
- ❏ b. something you already have.

8. Don Quixote said that the giants were evil and he had to fight them. The word *evil* means
- ❏ a. something good.
- ❏ b. something bad.

9. Don Quixote made promises to Sancho. A *promise* is
- ❏ a. an agreement to do something.
- ❏ b. a lie about something you have said that you will do.

Idioms

10. The giants turned into windmills. The idiom *turn into* means
- ❏ a. to go in a different direction.
- ❏ b. to change into something different.

How many questions did you answer correctly? Circle your score. Then fill in your score on the Score Chart on page 152.

Number Correct	1	2	3	4	5	6	7	8	9	10
Score	10	20	30	40	50	60	70	80	90	100

EXERCISES TO HELP YOU

Exercise A

Building sentences. Make sentences by adding the correct letter. The first one has been done for you.

1. Don Quixote read _____*c*_____   **a.** bought more books.
                                                   b. be his helper.

2. He sold some land and _____   **c.** books about knights.
                                                   d. to become a knight.

3. He decided _____

4. Sancho agreed to _____

Now write the sentences on the lines below. Begin each sentence with a capital letter. End it with a period.

1. _____

2. _____

3. _____

4. _____

Now do numbers 5–8 the same way.

5. The two men _____   **a.** saw something in a field ahead.

6. Don Quixote thought that he saw _____   **b.** that they were windmills.
                                                   c. giants with long arms.
                                                   d. went through one of the arms.

7. Sancho said _____

8. Don Quixote's lance _____

5. _____

6. _____

7. _____

8. _____

Exercise B

Understanding the story. Answer each question. Finish each sentence. Look back at the line numbers in the story. End each sentence with a period. The first one has been done for you.

1. Where did Don Quixote live?

He lived in a village in Spain.

_____

2. What did he read about in books?

He read about _____

_____ line 5

3. What did he start to have?

He started to have _____

_____ line 6

4. What did he want to look for?

He wanted to look for _____

_____ line 9

5. What did he make to wear?

He made _____

_____ line 10

6. What knocked Don Quixote off his horse?

The arm of a _____

knocked him off his horse. _____ line 29

Using the future tense with *will*. *Will* can be used to talk about future time. The contraction for *will* is *'ll*. Study the chart. Look at the contractions with *'ll*.

Future-Tense Verbs with *will*	
will + verb	*will* + verb
I will (I'll) run.	we will (we'll) run.
you will (you'll) run.	you will (you'll) run.
he will (he'll) run. she will (she'll) run. it will (it'll) run.	they will (they'll) run.
Will is often used for promises. Example: You say that you *will do* something in the future.	

Complete the sentences. They tell what will happen later in the story about Don Quixote. Use the future tense *will* with the verbs under the lines. The first one has been done for you.

1. Don Quixote ____*will have*____ many adventures.

have

2. Sancho thinks he _____ an island.

get

3. Don Quixote _____ many fights.

win

4. People _____ that he is crazy.

think

5. Someday Don Quixote _____ home. He will no longer think he is a knight.   return

Complete the sentences. These are promises from Don Quixote. Use the future tense *will* with the verbs under the lines.

6. Don Quixote said to Sancho, "We _____ many good deeds."

do

7. Don Quixote promised Sancho, "You _____ a reward."

receive

8. Don Quixote said, "Someone used magic. I _____ that person."

fight

Changing statements into questions. To change a statement into a question with the verb *to be,* put the verb first. Study the chart.

Statement	Don Quixote **was** from Spain.	There **were** windmills in the field.
Question	**Was** Don Quixote from Spain?	**Were** there windmills in the field?

Make these statements into questions. Put a question mark at the end of each question. The first one has been done for you.

1. Don Quixote was brave.

   Was Don Quixote brave?

2. Spain was Don Quixote's home.

   _____

3. His ideas were strange.

   _____

4. Sancho was Don Quixote's helper.

   _____

5. Land was a reward for knights.

   _____

6. There were giants in the field.

   _____

Exercise E
Understanding vocabulary. Match each word or phrase at the left with its meanings. Look back at the story. Write the letter in the blank. The first one has been done for you.

1. adventure ___c___
2. armor _____
3. good deed _____
4. lance _____
5. afraid of _____
6. agreed to _____

a. a metal suit that protects the body
b. said yes to
c. an exciting event
d. something you do to help others
e. a long, pointed weapon
f. scared of

Exercise F
Using vocabulary. Finish each sentence. Use the words and phrases next to the numbers in Exercise E. Write a word or phrase in each blank.

1. Don Quixote made promises to Sancho, and Sancho _____ be his helper.

2. Don Quixote made a suit of _____. He wore it.

3. Don Quixote said that Sancho didn't want to fight because he was _____ giants.

4. Don Quixote fought a windmill. His weapon was a _____.

5. Then Don Quixote wanted to start a new _____.

Exercise G

Speaking up. Look at the conversation. Practice it with a partner.

SHARING WITH OTHERS

Activity A

Readers Theater. Work in small groups. Imagine that your group is preparing a radio play. Practice reading the story aloud. One reader reads what Don Quixote says. Another reader reads what Sancho says. One or two narrators read the other words in the story.

Activity B

Sharing ideas. Everyone can learn by sharing ideas. Discuss these questions with a partner or with the group. Write your answer to one of the questions.

This story is famous. Why do you think people like it? What is your favorite part of the story? Why do you like that part of the story?

Do you like or admire Don Quixote? Why or why not?

Don Quixote followed his dream. Was this is a good idea? Why or why not?

BEGINNINGS

Long ago, people created stories to try to explain what happens in nature. These stories are called myths. Some myths tell how Earth began.

What stories do you know from other countries?

Do any of these stories tell what happens in nature?

How the World Began

a myth from Sumer

Sumer was an important land in western Asia about 3,000 years ago.

At the beginning of time, there were only wind and water.
A god decided to make a world. The god's name was Enlil.

One god wanted to stop Enlil. He did not want a world.
That god had a huge female dragon. The dragon's name was
5   Tiamat. She gathered an army of dragons. They came to fight
against Enlil.

Tiamat began to fight Enlil. She opened her **enormous** mouth.
Enlil asked the winds for help. Enlil **forced** all of the winds into
the dragon's mouth. Tiamat became larger and rounder. She
10   couldn't move.

With a knife, Enlil cut the dragon's body into two pieces. He
took one piece and put it down flat. It was the ground. Then he
took the other piece and formed it into an **arch.** He put it over
the ground. It was the sky. That is how Earth **came to be.**

How the World Began

a myth from Finland

In ancient Finland in northern Europe, people told this story about the beginning of the world.

At the beginning of time, there was only water. Above the water lived the goddess Air. Air had a daughter. The daughter's name was Ilmatar.

Ilmatar liked to **explore** the waters. One day she traveled far.
5 She decided to rest on the **surface** of the ocean. The wind started to blow hard. **Waves** rose around her. The storm lasted 700 years. After that, Ilmatar lived in the water all the time.

One day, Ilmatar was floating on her back. She bent one of her **knees.** A beautiful duck saw the knee. It landed on it. It laid
10 seven eggs there. The eggs became very hot. Ilmatar felt the heat from the eggs. She put her knee under the water. She wanted to cool it. The eggs fell to the bottom of the ocean.

Time passed. One of the eggs broke open. The bottom half of the **shell** became Earth. The top half of the shell became the
15 sky. The yellow **yolk** of the egg formed the sun. The white part of the egg became the moon and stars.

You can answer these questions

Put an *x* in the box next to the correct answer.

Reading Comprehension

1. In the myth from Sumer, Earth came from a dragon's
❑ a. body.
❑ b. egg.

2. In the myth from Sumer, Enlil was
❑ a. a god.
❑ b. a dragon.

3. Enlil asked for help from the
❑ a. waters.
❑ b. winds.

4. In the myth from Finland, Earth came from a
❑ a. goddess's knee.
❑ b. duck's egg.

5. Ilmatar was
❑ a. a goddess's daughter.
❑ b. the goddess Air.

6. Ilmatar liked to travel
❑ a. on the water.
❑ b. in the air.

Vocabulary

7. The dragon's mouth was enormous. The word *enormous* means
❑ a. big.
❑ b. ugly.

8. Ilmatar liked to explore the waters. When you *explore*, you
❑ a. forget where you are going.
❑ b. go to new places.

9. Ilmatar rested on the surface of the water. The word *surface* means
❑ a. the top part.
❑ b. a place for sitting.

Idioms

10. The two myths tell how Earth came to be. *Come to be* means
❑ a. begin.
❑ b. go someplace.

How many questions did you answer correctly? Circle your score. Then fill in your score on the Score Chart on page 152.

Number Correct	1	2	3	4	5	6	7	8	9	10
Score	10	20	30	40	50	60	70	80	90	100

EXERCISES TO HELP YOU

Exercise A
Building sentences. Make sentences by adding the correct letter. The first one has been done for you.

1. Enlil decided ___*c*___
2. The dragon's name _____
3. Enlil forced _____
4. Tiamat became _____

   a. larger and rounder.
   b. was Tiamat.
   c. to make a world.
   d. the winds into the dragon's mouth.

Now write the sentences on the lines below. Begin each sentence with a capital letter. End it with a period.

1. _____

2. _____

3. _____

4. _____

Now do numbers 5–8 the same way.

5. Ilmatar liked to _____
6. A duck laid _____
7. One of the eggs _____
8. The top half of the shell _____

   a. broke open.
   b. explore the waters.
   c. became the sky.
   d. seven eggs on Ilmatar's knee.

5. _____

6. _____

7. _____

8. _____

Exercise B

Understanding the myths. Answer each question. Finish each
sentence. Look back at the line numbers in the myths. End each
sentence with a period. The first one has been done for you.

Myth from Sumer

1. What was the name of the dragon?

   The name of the dragon was Tiamat.

2. What did Enlil force into the dragon's mouth?

   Enlil forced

   _____ lines 8–9, page 62

3. What did Enlil cut into two pieces?

   He cut

   _____ line 11, page 62

Myth from Finland

4. How many eggs did the duck lay on Ilmatar's knee?

   The duck laid

   _____ line 10, page 63

5. Where did the eggs fall?

   The eggs fell to

   _____ line 12, page 63

6. What did the bottom half of the eggshell become?

   The bottom half became

   _____ line 14, page 63

Exercise C

Using possessive nouns correctly. Possessive nouns in English end in *'s*. Possessive nouns tell about things that belong to someone or something. Study the chart below.

What Possessive Nouns Mean

Enlil's knife = Enlil has a knife; the knife belongs to Enlil.

The dragon's enormous mouth = The dragon has an enormous mouth.

Complete the sentences. Make a possessive noun from the word under each line. Write the possessives in the blanks. The first one has been done for you.

1. Enlil was a god. He had a plan.

   The _____*god's*_____ plan was to make a world.

   god

2. A dragon fought Enlil.

   The _____ name was Tiamat.

      dragon

3. Enlil cut the dragon's body into two pieces.

   The _____ two pieces formed the ground and the sky.

      body

4. The goddess Air had a daughter.

   The _____ name was Ilmatar.

      daughter

5. The duck laid seven eggs on Ilmatar's knee.

   The _____ eggs fell to the bottom of the ocean.

      duck

6. The shell of one of the eggs broke into two pieces.

   The _____ top half became the sky.

      shell

Exercise D

Using irregular past-tense verbs. Regular past-tense verbs end in *ed*. Irregular past-tense verbs do not end in *ed*. They have different forms.

Find the past tense of the irregular verbs shown below. Look in the myths on pages 62 and 63. Write the past-tense verbs in the blanks. The first one has been done for you.

Sumer myth

1. do   *did*
2. have   _ _ _
3. begin   _ _ _ _ _
4. take   _ _ _ _
5. cut   _ _ _

Finland myth

6. rise   _ _ _ _
7. bend   _ _ _ _
8. see   _ _ _
9. fall   _ _ _ _
10. break   _ _ _ _ _

Exercise E

Searching for past-tense verbs. Fourteen past-tense verbs are shown below. Some are regular. Others are irregular. Find each word in the puzzle and circle it. The words may appear sideways, up or down, diagonally, or backwards.

Verbs

decided	opened	saw
wanted	took	fell
had	cut	broke
came	put	became
asked	started	

```
D E A R N L H W M D A Z P L D
W E K U Q X L F E A P K L B Z
B M D V I D E T X P W O J L B
J E E I H O N D J A Y O E C I
S D C X C A B E F B E T N F H
W O H A W E T T O P E N E D V
X O Y F M W D R P J N K T C G
E K O R B E A A S R B N W K E
F W M D E R S T D C U V E T P
B T U O M I K S C O X U R E D
A E Q S P Q E N D U H A D E N
F L M K U T D S B L T F A E L
K K L A T J A A M S J Q X L R
Z V S R C W Y Z Z T L Q E X O
M L A V W V Q C F L L F K H P
```

Understanding vocabulary. Answer the riddles. Use the words in the box. Write the correct answer in the blank. The first one has been done for you.

arch enormous knee shell surface yolk

1. I am the yellow part of an egg.
   What am I? _____ *yolk* _____

2. I am the hard, outside part of the egg.
   What am I? _____

3. I mean the same thing as *big*.
   What am I? _____

4. I look like the top half of a circle.
   What am I? _____

5. I am the top part of things like oceans or tables.
   What am I? _____

6. I am part of your leg. I bend.
   What am I? _____

Exercise G
Speaking up. Look at the conversation. Practice it with a partner.

SHARING WITH OTHERS

Activity A

Telling the story in pictures. Draw three or four pictures to tell a myth. Use the myths in this book or other ones you know.

Here are some ideas:
Show what there was in the beginning.
Show the most important things that happened.
Show what there was at the end of the myth.

Activity B

Sharing ideas. Everyone can learn by sharing ideas. Discuss these questions with your partner or with the group. Write your answer to one of the questions.

What things are alike in the two myths?
What things are different?

Are these myths like any other myths you know?
How are they alike and different?

_____

_____

_____

_____

_____

_____

_____

_____

THE FARMER AND THE CIRCUS

What is it like to live on a farm?

What jobs do farmers do each day?

Have you ever seen a circus?

What might you see there?

The Farmer and the Circus

based on a story by Willa Cather

William Tavener and his family had a farm in Nebraska. William's sons helped him with the farmwork. His wife Hester cleaned and cooked, and she helped **to keep track of** their money.

William wanted to have a better farm than his neighbors had.
5 He was strict with his **sons.** He made them work hard. Hester felt sorry for her sons. She used her money to buy things for them.

One evening Hester and William were sitting in their **living room.** Hester was mending a sock. William was reading a newspaper. Hester's rocking chair was moving fast. She was **upset.**

10 Hester put the sock down. She said, "William, you should let the boys go to the circus tomorrow. They work hard. They need to have some fun. They've never been to a circus."

William put his newspaper down. He didn't say anything.

Hester continued. "The boys should learn about different things.
15 I went to the circus when I was little. I saw an elephant and some monkeys. I saw two camels. I will never forget the sight."

Hester didn't expect an answer from William. But he replied, "No, there was only one camel. The other was a dromedary."[1]

1. *dromedary:* a kind of camel with only one hump on its back.

Hester was **surprised.** "Why, I didn't know you were there, too!"

20 "Small boys do **foolish** things," William said. "I saved my money. Then I paid a boy to do my work for one day. I went to the circus, and I didn't tell my father."

"Oh, it didn't hurt anything," Hester said. "You always worked hard. I bet the circus **clown** made you laugh. Little boys like
25 clowns."

William leaned back in his chair. "I think I can still tell all of the clown's jokes," he said. "My new **boots** hurt my feet. But when that clown started to ride a donkey, I forgot about my **sore** feet."

Hester laughed. "I went to see the circus animals on their way to
30 town. They were getting water at a creek. The elephant filled his trunk with water. He sprayed water through the window of a house. It splashed a lady's dress."

Hester **realized** something. She and William talked about money too much. They didn't spend enough time talking about more
35 important things. That evening they talked about happy times in the past. Before William went to sleep, he gave some money to Hester. The money was for their sons' trip to the circus.

YOU CAN ANSWER THESE QUESTIONS

Put an *x* in the box next to the correct answer.

Reading Comprehension

1. William Tavener
   - ❑ a. made his sons work hard.
   - ❑ b. always gave his sons what they wanted.

2. Hester Tavener
   - ❑ a. did farmwork but didn't cook.
   - ❑ b. cooked, cleaned, and helped with the money.

3. At the start, Hester was
   - ❑ a. upset because her sons didn't have money for the circus.
   - ❑ b. happy because her family was together.

4. Hester thought that a circus was a place where children
   - ❑ a. spent money foolishly.
   - ❑ b. had fun and learned things.

5. When Hester and William were little,
   - ❑ a. they both went to a circus.
   - ❑ b. only Hester went to a circus.

6. Hester and William started to talk about
   - ❑ a. buying new socks.
   - ❑ b. good times in the past.

7. In the end, William gave Hester money. The money was for
   - ❑ a. tickets to the circus.
   - ❑ b. new clothes.

Vocabulary

8. William was strict with his sons. The word *strict* means
   - ❑ a. acting without thinking.
   - ❑ b. making sure that people follow rules.

9. Hester realized that she and William talked about money too much. The word *realize* means
   - ❑ a. suddenly understand.
   - ❑ b. try to do something.

Idioms

10. Hester helped to keep track of the money. The idiom *keep track of* means
    - ❑ a. try not to spend.
    - ❑ b. watch carefully.

How many questions did you answer correctly? Circle your score. Then fill in your score on the Score Chart on page 152.

Number Correct	1	2	3	4	5	6	7	8	9	10
Score	10	20	30	40	50	60	70	80	90	100

EXERCISES TO HELP YOU

Exercise A
Building sentences. Make sentences by adding the correct letter. The first one has been done for you.

1. The Taveners ___*d*___

2. The sons worked _____

3. The father was strict _____

4. Hester wanted her sons _____

    a. on the family farm.
    b. with his sons.
    c. to go to the circus.
    d. had a farm.

Now write the sentences on the lines below. Begin each sentence with a capital letter. End it with a period.

1. _____

2. _____

3. _____

4. _____

Do numbers 5–8 the same way.

5. Hester talked about _____

6. Her husband was _____

7. The couple talked _____

8. The father gave money _____

    a. at the same circus as she was.
    b. animals at the circus.
    c. about happy times in the past.
    d. for his sons' trip to the circus.

5. _____

6. _____

7. _____

8. _____

Exercise B

Understanding the story. Answer each question. Finish each sentence. Look back at the line numbers in the story. End each sentence with a period. The first one has been done for you.

1. Where did William Tavener have a farm?

   William Tavener had a farm in Nebraska.

   _____

2. With whom was William strict?

   William was strict with _____

   _____ line 5

3. What did Hester say that the boys needed?

   Hester said that the boys needed to _____

   _____ line 12

4. When did Hester say she went to the circus?

   Hester said, "I went to the circus when _____

   _____ line 15

5. What did the clown help William to forget?

   The clown helped William to forget _____

   _____ line 28

6. What did William give Hester money for?

   William gave Hester money for _____

   _____ line 37

Exercise C

Using pronouns correctly. Pronouns may follow action verbs or prepositions. Such pronouns are called object pronouns. Study this chart of object pronouns.

Object Pronouns	
Singular	**Plural**
me	us
you	you
him	them
her	
it	

Examples: Hester gave *him* the money.
　　　　　William got the money from *her.*

Fill in the blanks. Use the correct object pronouns to replace the underlined words. The first one has been done for you.

1. William's sons helped <u>their father</u> on the farm.
   They helped ____*him*____ with the farm work.

2. Hester cleaned and cooked in <u>the house</u>.
   She did a lot of work in _____.

3. William gave money to <u>Hester</u> for things for the house.
   He also gave money to _____ for things for herself.

4. Hester was in the living room with <u>her husband</u>.
   She started to talk to _____.

5. She said, "The boys help <u>you and me</u>. They help
   _____ a lot."

6. Hester gave the money to <u>the boys</u>. She gave the money to
   _____.

Exercise D
Using verbs followed by infinitives. Infinitives are verb forms that start with the word *to*. For example, *to be, to have,* and *to do* are infinitives. Study the chart below. It shows verbs followed by infinitives.

need + infinitive	Hester *needed* **to get** some money.
want + infinitive	William *wanted* **to have** the best farm.
start + infinitive	The clown *started* **to ride** a donkey.

Read each sentence below. Read the verbs under the lines. Then write each sentence on the line provided. Write the first verb in the past tense. Write the second verb in the infinitive form. The first sentence has been done for you.

1. The boys _____ to the circus.
   want / go

   The boys wanted to go to the circus.

2. They _____ money.
   need / get

   _____

3. Hester _____ to her husband.
   start / speak

   _____

4. Hester _____ money to the boys.
   want / give

   _____

5. Hester and William _____ about happy times.
   start / talk

   _____

6. Hester thought they _____ less about money.
   need / talk

   _____

Exercise E

Adding an adjective. Read each sentence below. Think about which adjective belongs in that sentence. Write the letter of the adjective on the blank in the sentence. The first one has been done for you.

1. At first, Hester was ____a____ because she wanted William to let the boys go to the circus.

2. Hester was _____ when her husband said something about the camels.

3. They both were at the same circus when they were _____ .

4. William had _____ feet, but he still enjoyed the circus.

5. Hester understood that little boys often do _____ things.

a. upset
b. little
c. sore
d. surprised
e. foolish

Exercise F

Understanding vocabulary. Answer the riddles. Use the words in the box. Write the correct answer in each blank.

boots	clown	camel	living room	neighbors

1. I make people laugh.
   What am I? _____

2. I am the people who live near you.
   What am I? _____

3. I am a place in a house where people sit. Often I have a TV.
   What am I? _____

4. I am an animal with two humps on its back.
   What am I? _____

5. I am something you wear on your feet.
   What am I? _____

Speaking up. Look at the conversation. Practice it with a partner.

SHARING WITH OTHERS

Activity A
Word game. Write clues for words from the story.

1. Work with a partner. Together, choose five words from the story.
2. Write a clue for each word.

Examples:
This has news. People read it every day.
(Answer: newspaper)

This is a special chair. It can move.
(Answer: rocking chair)

Activity B
Sharing ideas. Everyone can learn by sharing ideas. Discuss these questions with your partner or with the group. Write your answers to one of the questions.

What problem did Hester have at the start?
How did she solve it?

What was important to William? How do you know?

What lesson did Hester and William learn from their conversation?

PERSEUS

Many famous myths come from ancient Greece.

Think about any heroes you know from Greek myths.

What is a hero?

What does someone do to be a hero?

Perseus

a Greek myth

Acrisius was a king in Greece. He asked a prophet about his
future. A prophet is someone who tells what will happen. The
prophet said, "One day your grandson will kill you." At the time,
the grandson was just a baby. His name was Perseus.

5 Acrisius put Perseus into a large box. He also put Danae,
Perseus's mother, into the box. He put the box into the ocean.
The waves carried the box to an island. There Perseus **grew into**
a young man.

Polydectes was the king of the island. Polydectes wanted to
10 marry Perseus's mother. Perseus did not want Polydectes to be
his mother's husband. Polydectes wanted to **get rid of** Perseus.
He gave Perseus a **challenge:** "Kill the monster Medusa." Perseus
agreed to do the difficult task. He was a brave young man.

Medusa had once been a beautiful woman with **lovely**, long hair.
15 She had said that she was more beautiful than the goddesses.
The gods were angry and punished her. She became a **hideous**
monster with snakes for hair. She was ugly, but she had a strange
power. When anyone looked at her, that person turned to stone.

The gods decided to help Perseus. They gave him a **shiny** round
20 shield and a sword.

After a long journey, Perseus arrived at Medusa's home. He said to himself, "I have to be careful. I can't look at the monster. I don't want to turn to stone."

He thought of a plan. He **listened for** the sound of the snakes in Medusa's hair. Finally he heard a hissing sound. He was near the monster!

"Now what do I do? I can't look at her. How can I kill her?" Then he saw the light of the sun. The light was coming off his shield. He said, "I can use my shield as a mirror. I will hold it up and see Medusa's face on it. I won't have to look at her." He moved ahead. He saw Medusa in his shield. She was sleeping. He cut off her head.

Perseus returned to the island. He gave Medusa's head to Polydectes. Polydectes made a **fatal** mistake. He looked at the head, and he died.

What happened to Perseus's grandfather? One day Perseus **took part in** some games. He threw a flat and round piece of metal called a discus. The wind caught the discus. The discus hit an old man. It killed him. The man was Acrisius. So in the end, the prophet's words were true. Acrisius did not escape his **fate.**

YOU CAN ANSWER THESE QUESTIONS

Put an *x* in the box next to the correct answer.

Reading Comprehension

1. Acrisius was worried that
   - ❏ a. he was growing old.
   - ❏ b. his grandson was going to kill him.

2. Polydectes wanted to
   - ❏ a. look at a monster.
   - ❏ b. marry Perseus's mother.

3. Medusa had said that she was
   - ❏ a. stronger than the goddesses.
   - ❏ b. more beautiful than the goddesses.

4. Medusa was able to change people into
   - ❏ a. snakes.
   - ❏ b. stone.

5. Perseus used his shield
   - ❏ a. to see Medusa.
   - ❏ b. to hear snakes.

6. At the end, Perseus killed
   - ❏ a. Acrisius.
   - ❏ b. Polydectes.

Vocabulary

7. The brave Perseus agreed to Polydectes's challenge. The word *challenge* means
   - ❏ a. something hard to do.
   - ❏ b. a short journey.

8. Medusa once had lovely, long hair. The word *lovely* means
   - ❏ a. thin.
   - ❏ b. pretty.

9. Acrisius did not escape his fate. The word *fate* means
   - ❏ a. what is going to happen.
   - ❏ b. the anger of the gods.

Idioms

10. Acrisius wanted to get rid of Perseus. When you *get rid of* something, you
    - ❏ a. make it go away.
    - ❏ b. find it and keep it.

How many questions did you answer correctly? Circle your score. Then fill in your score on the Score Chart on page 153.

Number Correct	1	2	3	4	5	6	7	8	9	10
Score	10	20	30	40	50	60	70	80	90	100

Exercises to Help You

Exercise A

Building sentences. Make sentences by adding the correct
letter. The first one has been done for you.

1. Acrisius asked a prophet
   _____*d*_____

2. Perseus grew _____

3. Polydectes asked Perseus to

   _____

4. The brave Perseus _____

a. agreed to the king's
   challenge.
b. kill a monster.
c. into a brave young man.
d. about the future.

Now write the sentences on the lines below. Begin each
sentence with a capital letter. End it with a period.

1. _____

2. _____

3. _____

4. _____

Now do numbers 5–8 the same way.

5. Perseus thought _____

6. Perseus listened for _____

7. Perseus used his
   shield _____

8. Acrisius could not _____

a. the sound of the snakes.
b. escape his fate.
c. of a plan.
d. as a mirror.

5. _____

6. _____

7. _____

8. _____

Exercise B

Understanding the story. Answer each question. Finish each
sentence. Look back at the line numbers in the story. End each
sentence with a period. The first one has been done for you.

1. Who was Perseus's grandfather?

   Perseus's grandfather was Acrisius.

2. Whose mother did Polydectes want to marry?

   He wanted to

   _____ line 10

3. What did Polydectes ask Perseus to do?

   He asked Perseus to

   _____ line 12

4. What power did Medusa have?

   She turned people

   _____ line 18

5. Perseus was near Medusa. What did he hear?

   He heard

   _____ line 25

6. How did Perseus kill Medusa?

   He cut

   _____ lines 31–32

Exercise C

Using possessive pronouns correctly. Some possessive pronouns are used as adjectives. They describe nouns. Other possessive pronouns are used as nouns. Study the chart below.

Possessive Pronouns Used as Adjectives		Possessive Pronouns Used as Nouns	
Singular	*Plural*	*Singular*	*Plural*
my	our	mine	ours
your	your	yours	yours
his	their	his	theirs
her		hers	
its		its	

Examples: *Your* car is blue. The car is *yours*.

Fill in the blanks. Use possessive pronouns as adjectives. The first one has been done for you.

1. Acrisius was a king. ____*His*____ grandson was Perseus.

2. Danae and _____ son Perseus came to an island.

3. Polydectes told Perseus, "I want to marry Danae, _____ mother."

4. The goddesses were proud of _____ beauty. They punished Medusa.

Fill in the blanks. Use possessive pronouns as nouns. The first one is done for you.

5. The gods gave Perseus a shield. The special shield was ____*his*____.

6. The gods told Perseus, "Please take your shield from the group of shields over there. _____ is the shiny shield."

7. Perseus said, "I agreed to kill the monster. The job is _____."

Exercise D

Adding an adjective. Complete each of the sentences by adding the correct adjective. Use each adjective once.

1. Polydectes looked at Medusa's head and died. He made a _____ mistake.

   brave

2. Perseus accepted Polydectes's challenge. He was _____.

   lovely

3. Medusa's hair was once long and _____.

   shiny

4. Medusa became a _____ monster.

   hideous

5. The gods gave Perseus a _____ shield.

   fatal

Exercise E

Putting words in the correct order. Make sentences by putting the words in the correct order. Write each sentence on the line. The first one has been done for you.

1. Polydectes / asked / monster / kill / to / a / Perseus

   Polydectes asked Perseus to kill a monster.

2. Polydectes's / accepted / Perseus / challenge

   _____.

3. decided / to / help / The / gods / Perseus

   _____.

4. sound / hissing / Perseus / heard / a

   _____.

5. Perseus / head / Medusa's / returned / with

   _____.

6. old / discus / an / man / hit / The

   _____.

Exercise F

Understanding vocabulary. Many verbs can go together with other words to make phrases. Study the verb phrases at the left. Match them with their meanings. Write the correct letter in the blank.

1. grew into _____

2. get rid of _____

3. listened for _____

4. thought of _____

5. took part in _____

a. waited to hear

b. became; changed into

c. had a new idea

d. did something with others; joined in

e. make someone or something go away

Exercise G

Using vocabulary. Complete the sentences with the phrases from Exercise F. Use each phrase once.

1. King Acrisius wanted to _____ Perseus. The king put him into a box and put the box in the ocean.

2. The baby Perseus _____ a brave young man.

3. Perseus _____ a plan to kill Medusa.

4. Perseus _____ the sound of snakes.

5. Perseus _____ some games. He threw the discus.

Exercise H

Speaking up. Look at the conversations. Practice them with a partner.

SHARING WITH OTHERS

Activity A

Putting the story in order. Do all five steps of this activity.

1. Choose five sentences from different parts of the story.
2. Write each sentence down on a separate piece of paper.
3. Work with a partner. Give your partner your sentences.
4. Put the sentences you have in order. Put first the sentence found first in the story. Put next the sentence found second in the story. Continue in this way.
5. Check your partner's sentences. Are they in the correct order?

Activity B

Sharing ideas. Everyone can learn by sharing ideas. Discuss these questions with your partner or with the group. Write your answer to one of the questions.

Which words do you think describe Perseus?

brave
smart
foolish
lucky

1. Do you think that Perseus is a hero? Why or why not?

2. Do you think that you can escape your fate? Why or why not?

Choose one of the questions. Write your answer below.

_____

_____

_____

_____

_____

_____

APPLES, APPLES

Nature gives us many wonderful fruits and vegetables to eat.
How many fruits and vegetables can you name?
What is your favorite fruit?
What is your favorite vegetable?

Mountain Mary

an American legend

*Mountain Mary and Johnny Appleseed are folk heroes to people in the United States. Both lived about 200 years ago. Both loved nature. Both left a **legacy** for others who lived after them. People today still tell stories about them.*

5　Everyone called her Mountain Mary. Her real name was Mary Young. She lived in the hills of eastern Pennsylvania. She lived alone, but she had many friends. Many people knew her. Mountain Mary was an **expert** on plants called herbs. She used herbs to make medicine.

10　Mountain Mary was kind and **generous.** She especially **cared about** animals. Sometimes animals ate the plants in her garden. She didn't try to hurt the animals. First she caught them. She took them high up in the hills. Then she set them free.

Mountain Mary especially loved apples. One time she cut off
15　parts of two apple trees. She grew the parts together as one tree. In this way, she created a new kind of apple. Its name was the Good Mary. Mary Young died in 1819 at the age of 70. After she died, a neighbor said, "There is one less **saint** on Earth."

Johnny Appleseed

an American legend

People called him Johnny Appleseed. His real name was John Chapman. He lived in the Ohio River Valley. He walked from place to place through the **countryside.** He didn't have a home. He carried only a few things with him. One thing was a **sack** of apple seeds. Johnny walked through the forests to small towns and farms. He planted many apple seeds. The seeds grew into trees. In this way, Johnny gave a great gift to others. From his trees, people had apples for many years.

Johnny sometimes **exchanged** small apple trees for things he needed. In this way, he got food and clothes for himself.

Johnny met many people as he walked. Sometimes he helped to end **arguments.** People respected him. He was fair.

Johnny loved animals. One night he was cooking his food over a fire. He saw moths flying into the fire. This made him sad. He didn't want the moths to die. He didn't like to hurt living things. So he **put out** the fire. That night Johnny was cold. He ate uncooked food. By his action, he showed his great love for nature. Johnny Appleseed died in 1845 at the age of 71.

YOU CAN ANSWER THESE QUESTIONS

Put an *x* in the box next to the correct answer.

Reading Comprehension

1. The stories about Mountain Mary and Johnny Appleseed
   - ❏ a. are true.
   - ❏ b. are not true.

2. Mountain Mary and Johnny Appleseed
   - ❏ a. lived in the past.
   - ❏ b. live today.

3. Both Mountain Mary and Johnny Appleseed
   - ❏ a. loved nature.
   - ❏ b. loved cities.

4. Both Mountain Mary and Johnny Appleseed liked
   - ❏ a. to grow plants.
   - ❏ b. to make medicine.

5. Both Mountain Mary and Johnny Appleseed moved from place to place.
   - ❏ a. true
   - ❏ b. false

Vocabulary

6. Mountain Mary and Johnny Appleseed left a legacy for others who lived after them. A *legacy* is
   - ❏ a. a big garden.
   - ❏ b. something you give to children or other younger people.

7. Mountain Mary was kind and generous. The word *generous* means
   - ❏ a. behaving well.
   - ❏ b. willing to share with others.

8. A neighbor said that there was one less saint. The word *saint* means
   - ❏ a. a good and holy person.
   - ❏ b. a person who works on a farm.

9. Johnny Appleseed exchanged apple trees for other things. *Exchanged* means
   - ❏ a. gave something and got back something else.
   - ❏ b. made something look different.

Idioms

10. The idiom *care about* means
    - ❏ a. like something or someone very much and want to help.
    - ❏ b. help to grow a plant from when it is small.

How many questions did you answer correctly? Circle your score. Then fill in your score on the Score Chart on page 153.

Number Correct	1	2	3	4	5	6	7	8	9	10
Score	10	20	30	40	50	60	70	80	90	100

EXERCISES TO HELP YOU

Exercise A

Building sentences. Make sentences by adding the correct letter. The first one has been done for you.

1. Mountain Mary _____*b*_____

2. Mountain Mary cared _____

3. She refused _____

4. She created _____

    a. a new kind of apple.
    b. lived about two hundred years ago.
    c. to hurt animals.
    d. about animals.

Now write the sentences on the lines below. Begin each sentence with a capital letter. End it with a period.

1. _____

2. _____

3. _____

4. _____

Now do numbers 5–8 the same way.

5. Johnny Appleseed walked _____

6. He planted _____

7. Sometimes he helped to _____

8. Johnny didn't like _____

    a. from place to place.
    b. end arguments.
    c. many apple seeds.
    d. to hurt a living thing.

5. _____

6. _____

7. _____

8. _____

Exercise B

Understanding the story. Answer each question. Finish each sentence. Look back at the line numbers in the stories. End each sentence with a period. The first one has been done for you.

1. When did the two people in the stories live?

   They lived about two hundred years ago.

2. Where did the two people in the stories live?

   Mountain Mary lived in _____,

   and Johnny Appleseed lived in _____

   _____ line 6, page 92; line 2, page 93

3. What was Mountain Mary's real name?

   Her _____

   _____ lines 5–6, page 92

4. What did Mountain Mary create?

   She created _____

   _____ line 16, page 92

5. Where did Johnny Appleseed walk?

   He walked _____

   _____ line 3, page 93

6. What did Johnny Appleseed carry with him?

   He carried a sack _____

   _____ lines 4–5, page 93

Exercise C

Using negatives with the past tense. Most negative sentences are formed with the word *not*. Negative sentences in the past tense have *did not* or *didn't* before the verb. The verb is in the base form. Read the chart below.

Base Form	Past Tense	Negative in the Past Tense
have	had	didn't have
live	lived	didn't live
eat	ate	didn't eat

Here are some examples. These sentences have *didn't* before the base form of the verb.

Mountain Mary *didn't have* any children.
Johnny Appleseed *didn't buy* a house.

Complete the sentences below. Change the underlined verb to the base form. Use *didn't* to make the sentence negative. The first one has been done for you.

1. Mountain Mary ___*didn't live*___ in England. She <u>lived</u> in the United States.

2. Mountain Mary _____ apples to make medicine. She <u>used</u> herbs to make medicine.

3. Mountain Mary _____ to kill the animals she caught. She <u>wanted</u> to set them free.

4. Johnny Appleseed _____ from place to place in the city. He <u>walked</u> from place to place in the country.

5. Johnny Appleseed _____ much money. He <u>had</u> only a few things.

6. Johnny Appleseed _____ to start arguments. He <u>wanted</u> to end arguments.

Exercise D

Using past-tense verbs. Change the verbs below to past tense. You can find the past tenses on pages 92 and 93. Write the past-tense verb on the line provided. Then find the past-tense verbs in the puzzle. The words appear up and down or sideways. Circle them.

Page 92

catch _____

grow _____

know _____

leave _____

say _____

Page 93

call _____

carry _____

love _____

plant _____

walk _____

C	O	P	L	A	N	T	E	D
A	G	R	E	W	O	N	E	E
U	Q	Z	F	C	P	N	R	W
G	I	C	T	B	J	L	H	A
H	C	A	R	R	I	E	D	L
T	O	L	D	X	S	N	K	K
C	R	L	E	B	W	U	N	E
O	Q	E	M	L	O	V	E	D
O	T	D	S	A	I	D	W	Z

Exercise E

Using the past tense. Complete the sentences. Use past-tense verbs from Exercise D.

1. Both Mountain Mary and Johnny Appleseed _____ a legacy for future generations.

2. Both Mountain Mary and Johnny Appleseed _____ nature.

3. Mary _____ the animals in her garden, but she didn't kill them.

4. She _____ parts of different apple trees together.

5. His real name was John Chapman, but everyone _____ him Johnny Appleseed.

Exercise F

Adding vocabulary. On the left are six words or idioms from the story. Complete each sentence by adding the correct word or idiom.

1. Johnny Appleseed and Mountain Mary left a
_____. They left many plants
for people.They showed that nature
is important.

   cared about

2. Mary liked and helped people and animals.
She _____ them.

   countryside

3. Mary used herbs to make medicine.
She was an _____ on herbs.

   expert

4. Johnny Appleseed walked through
the _____ .

   legacy

5. Johnny _____ small apple trees
for food and clothing.

   put out

6. Johnny _____ his fire so that
the moths would not die.

   exchanged

Exercise G

Speaking up. Look at the conversation. Practice it with
a partner.

SHARING WITH OTHERS

Activity A
Making riddles. Follow the directions.

1. Work with a partner. Write five statements. In each statement, tell about Mountain Mary, Johnny Appleseed, or both.

Examples:
I lived two hundred years ago. (both)
I lived in the Ohio River Valley. (Johnny Appleseed)
I had an herb garden. (Mountain Mary)

2. Work with another pair of students. Read your clues to the pair. How many riddles do the students guess right? Then listen as the other two students read their clues to you. How many can you guess right?

Activity B
Sharing ideas. Everyone can learn by sharing ideas. Discuss these questions with your partner or with the group. Write your answer to one of the questions.

What was the legacy of Mountain Mary?

What was the legacy of Johnny Appleseed?

Who are some famous people in the history of a country you know?

Why are these people famous?

Do other people respect them? Why?

_____

_____

_____

_____

_____

THE NEGLECTED GRANDFATHER

This story is about an old man and his family. Some people in the family are not kind to the old man. They neglect him.

How do you feel about old people?

Do you enjoy visiting them?

The Neglected Grandfather

a Mexican folktale

Many years ago in Mexico, an old couple lived in a village. The village was in a valley between high mountains. There were many farms around the village. The old man and his wife were poor. They did not have much land. One winter when it was very cold, the old woman became sick and died. The old man went to live with his son's family on a nearby farm.

For several years, the old man **often** was able to help his son with work on the farm. Then one day the old man was badly hurt. He was taking care of a horse, and the horse kicked him. The horse broke the old man's hip. The old man did not get better, and he was not able to walk.

The son had a **wife** and one child, a teenage boy. At first the family took good care of the **grandfather.** Everyone lived in **harmony.**

After a while, however, the wife grew tired of the old man. She said he always was **in the way.** The son and his wife moved the old man into a barn.

In the barn, the grandfather often was **neglected**. He **usually** did not get much food to eat. He **frequently** did not have warm clothes to wear.

One winter day, the teenage boy went to visit his grandfather in the barn. "My grandson," the old man said. "Please find a blanket for me. It is very cold today, and I am **freezing**."

The boy looked around the barn, but he could find only a small rug. He took the rug to his father and mother.

"Mother, I need a pair of scissors," the boy said. "My grandfather is cold, and I **am going to** give him half of this rug to use as a blanket."

"Why aren't you going to give him the whole rug?" the father asked his son.

"Because, father, I want to save half of the rug for you. You will need it when you are old and you move into the barn."

The father felt ashamed. He allowed the old man to move back into the house. Once again the family took good care of the grandfather.

YOU CAN ANSWER THESE QUESTIONS

Put an *x* in the box next to the correct answer.

Reading Comprehension

1. The old man and his wife were
   - ❏ **a.** poor.
   - ❏ **b.** rich.

2. At first the grandfather went to live
   - ❏ **a.** in the barn.
   - ❏ **b.** in his son's house.

3. After the grandfather moved into the barn,
   - ❏ **a.** his grandson never visited him.
   - ❏ **b.** he was neglected.

4. The grandson wanted to
   - ❏ **a.** change a blanket into a rug.
   - ❏ **b.** cut a rug into two pieces.

5. The man decided to be nicer to his father when the boy showed him that
   - ❏ **a.** one day the man, too, would be old.
   - ❏ **b.** the wife was right.

6. At the end, the family
   - ❏ **a.** moved to a bigger house.
   - ❏ **b.** all lived together.

Vocabulary

7. At first the family lived in harmony. *Harmony* means
   - ❏ **a.** peace.
   - ❏ **b.** a city.

8. In the barn, the grandfather was neglected. *Neglected* means
   - ❏ **a.** not moved.
   - ❏ **b.** not helped.

9. The grandfather said that he was freezing. *Freezing* means
   - ❏ **a.** very hungry.
   - ❏ **b.** very cold.

Idioms

10. The wife thought that the grandfather was in the way. The idiom *in the way* means
   - ❏ **a.** causing difficulty for other people.
   - ❏ **b.** telling others what to do.

How many questions did you answer correctly? Circle your score. Then fill in your score on the Score Chart on page 153.

Number Correct	1	2	3	4	5	6	7	8	9	10
Score	10	20	30	40	50	60	70	80	90	100

EXERCISES TO HELP YOU

Exercise A

Building sentences. Make sentences by adding the correct letter.
The first one has been done for you.

1. An old couple _____C_____

    a. the old man's hip.
    b. a barn.

2. The horse broke _____

    c. lived in a village.
    d. of the old man.

3. The wife grew tired _____

4. The old man was
moved into _____

Now write the sentences on the lines below. Begin each
sentence with a capital letter. End it with a period.

1. _____

2. _____

3. _____

4. _____

Now do numbers 5–8 the same way.

5. The grandfather often _____

    a. to visit his grandfather.
    b. was neglected.

6. The teenage boy went _____

    c. to move back into the house.

7. The boy looked around _____

    d. the barn.

8. The father allowed the old man _____

5. _____

6. _____

7. _____

8. _____

    _____

Exercise B

Understanding the story. Answer each question. Finish each sentence. Look back at the line numbers in the stories. End each sentence with a period. The first one has been done for you.

1. Where did the old man and the old woman live?

   They lived in a village.

   _____.

2. What did a horse do to the old man?

   The horse broke the _____

   _____ line 10

3. What happened to the old man when he was in the barn?

   In the barn, the grandfather often _____

   _____ line 18

4. What did the grandfather ask the boy to find?

   He asked the boy _____

   _____ lines 22–23

5. What did the boy ask his mother for?

   He asked her for _____

   _____ line 26

6. Why didn't the boy want to take the entire rug?

   _____ *to save half for when his father*

   was as old as the grandfather. _____ line 31

Exercise C

Using *to be* + *going to* as a future tense. The present tense of the verb *to be* can be used with the phrase *going to* for talking about the future. The verb form looks like this: *to be* + *going to* + main verb.

Examples:

> The boy in the story said, "My grandfather is cold, and I <u>am going to give</u> him half of this rug to use as a blanket."
> "Why <u>aren't</u> you <u>going to give</u> him the whole rug?" the father asked his son.

Study the chart.

I am going to _____	we are going to _____
you are going to _____	you are going to _____
he is going to _____ she is going to _____ it is going to _____	they are going to _____

Complete the sentences. Use the correct form of *to be* + *going to* with the verb under the line. The first one has been done for you.

1. The wife told her husband, "The old man *is going to move*
    out of our house."
    move

2. The father told the grandfather, "You _____
    in the barn."
    live

3. The grandfather told the grandson, "They _____
    me."
    neglect

4. The grandson said to the grandfather, "I _____
    for a blanket."
    look

5. The grandson said to the father, "You _____
    half of this rug."
    need

6. At the end, the father said, "In the future, we _____
    together."
    be

Using adverbs of frequency. Adverbs of frequency tell how often things happen. Some things happen every day. Other things happen once a year.

Here are some adverbs of frequency:

always usually often frequently sometimes never

If you think about someone's weekly schedule, it can help you to understand adverbs of frequency. Here are some examples:

Maria helps her parents with housework seven days a week.
Maria **always** helps her parents with housework.

Maria reads a book in the afternoon five days a week.
Maria **usually** reads a book in the afternoon.

Maria has swimming practice three days a week.
Maria **often** has swimming practice.
Maria **frequently** has swimming practice.

Maria baby-sits in the evening one or two days a week.
Maria **sometimes** baby-sits in the evening.

Note: *never* = zero days a week

Complete the sentences about the story. Use adverbs.

1. The old man helped his son with farmwork three days a week.
   The old man _____ helped his son with farmwork.

2. The wife says that the grandfather is in the way seven days a week.
   The wife says that the grandfather is _____ in the way.

3. The boy visits his grandfather one or two days a week.
   The boy _____ visits his grandfather.

4. The grandfather does not get much food five days a week.
   The grandfather _____ does not get much food.

5. The family should neglect the old man zero days a week.
   The family should _____ neglect the old man.

Exercise E

Understanding family words. Use the family words in the box to complete the sentences.

son	wife	grandfather	grandson	father

Write the correct word in the blank.

1. The old man helped his _____ with work on the farm.

2. The son's _____ grew tired of the old man.

3. The son moved his _____ to the barn.

4. The teenage boy went to visit his _____ in the barn.

5. The teenage boy is the old man's _____.

Exercise F

Using words with the same or opposite meanings. Some of the pairs of words in the story have opposite meanings, and some have the same meaning. For each pair of words below, write *O* for *opposite* or *S* for *same*.

1. high   low   _____

2. harmony   peace   _____

3. neglected   took care of   _____

4. warm   cold   _____

5. ashamed   sorry   _____

Exercise G

Speaking up. Look at the conversation. Practice it with a partner.

SHARING WITH OTHERS

Activity A

1. Which of the following ideas do you think best explains the lesson? Which idea is most important for your own family? Share your opinion with a partner or a group.

   a. Families need to live in harmony.
   b. We should be nice to everyone in our family.
   c. We need to take good care of old people in our family; they once took care of us.

2. Which person do you like best in the story? Why?

   a. the grandfather   **b.** the father   **c.** the grandson

---

Activity B

Sharing ideas. Everyone can learn by sharing ideas. Discuss these questions with your partner or with the group. Write your answer to one of the questions.

1. You learn things from older members of your family. What are some things that you have learned outside school this year?

2. Tell about how you think older people should be treated. What are some things older people might need help with?

THE GIFT OF THE MAGI

PART ONE

This story is about a wife and a husband who want to get special gifts for each other.

What do you do when you have to buy a special gift? How do you decide what to buy?

What is a special gift someone gave you?

The Gift of the Magi

based on a story by O. Henry

One dollar and eighty-seven cents. That was all. Della counted the money carefully. She counted it three times. The **total** was the same. And the next day was Christmas. She wanted to buy a nice gift for her husband, Jim, but that was all the money she had.

5   Della sat down on the old **couch** and cried quietly. Like the couch, the apartment was not in the best condition. At the front door was a bell. It didn't ring. And near the bell was a card. It had the name "Mr. and Mrs. James Dillingham Young."

Della had thought about the gift for many happy hours. She
10   wanted something fine and **rare.** She wanted something very special for Jim, because he was a very special person. Suddenly she went before the mirror. Her eyes were shining brightly, but her face had lost its color. Rapidly she pulled down her hair.

Now, Mr. and Mrs. James Dillingham Young were very proud of
15   two of their **possessions.** One was Della's hair. The other was Jim's gold watch. It had been his father's and his grandfather's.

Della put her hair up again fast. She stood still for a few seconds. A tear splashed on the **worn** red carpet. Then she put on her old brown jacket and hat. She hurried down the stairs to the street.

20 She stopped at a sign. It said "Madame Sofronie. We Buy Hair."
Della went inside the shop. "Will you buy my hair?" asked Della.

"Take your hat off and let's have a look at it," said Madame. Della
pulled down her hair. "Twenty dollars," said Madame.

"Do it **quickly**," said Della.

25 The next two hours went by fast for Della. She was looking in
stores for Jim's present. She found it **at last**! It surely was the
perfect gift for Jim. It was a simple platinum watch chain. Its
value was in its rich **material** and its simple design. But it was
special—like The Watch. And it was like Jim—quiet and **solid.**
30 She paid twenty-one dollars for the watch chain. Then she
hurried home with 87 cents. Della felt very pleased with the gift.

When Della reached home, she got out her curling irons. She
started to **fix** her hair. Soon her head was covered with tiny curls.

At 7 o'clock the coffee was made. The pan for the chops was on
35 the stove.

Jim was never late. Della heard his step on the stair. Her face
turned white for just a moment. "What is he going to think about
my hair?" she thought.

YOU CAN ANSWER THESE QUESTIONS

Put an *x* in the box next to the correct answer.

Reading Comprehension

1. Mr. and Mrs. James Dillingham Young
- ❏ a. had a lot of money.
- ❏ b. didn't have much money.

2. Della was
- ❏ a. Jim's wife.
- ❏ b. Jim's mother.

3. Della wanted to buy
- ❏ a. a special gift for her husband.
- ❏ b. some chops for her husband.

4. Della decided to
- ❏ a. sell her hair.
- ❏ b. sell some furniture.

5. Della bought
- ❏ a. a watch chain.
- ❏ b. a curling iron.

6. Della spent
- ❏ a. twenty-one dollars for the gift.
- ❏ b. eighty-seven cents for the gift.

7. At the end of part one, Della had
- ❏ a. long and straight hair.
- ❏ b. short and curly hair.

Vocabulary

8. Della counted the money, and the total was only $1.87. The word *total* means
- ❏ a. all of something.
- ❏ b. part of something.

9. The couple had two special possessions. The words *possessions* means
- ❏ a. expensive things.
- ❏ b. things that people own.

Idioms

10. Della found Jim's present at last. The idiom *at last* means
- ❏ a. after a long time.
- ❏ b. at the end of the day.

How many questions did you answer correctly? Circle your score. Then fill in your score on the Score Chart on page 153.

Number Correct	1	2	3	4	5	6	7	8	9	10
Score	10	20	30	40	50	60	70	80	90	100

EXERCISES TO HELP YOU

Exercise A

Building sentences. Make sentences by adding the correct letter. The first one has been done for you.

1. Della counted ___c___

2. She sat on the couch _____

3. She wanted to _____

4. She pulled _____

a. down her hair.
b. buy a gift for her husband.
c. her money.
d. and cried.

Now write the sentences on the lines below. Begin each sentence with a capital letter. End it with a period.

1. _____

2. _____

3. _____

4. _____

Now do numbers 5-8 the same way.

5. Della sold _____

6. She looked in _____

7. She paid _____

8. She hurried _____

a. her hair.
b. home with her gift.
c. the stores for a present.
d. twenty-one dollars for the watch chain.

5. _____

6. _____

7. _____

8. _____

Exercise B

Understanding the story. Answer each question. Finish each sentence. Look back at the line numbers in the stories. End each sentence with a period. The first one has been done for you.

1. How much money did Della have at first?

She had one dollar and eighty-seven cents.

_____

2. What did she want to buy?

She wanted to buy _____

_____ lines 3–4

3. What was one thing that Della was proud of?

She _____

_____ line 15

4. What did Della decide to sell?

She decided _____

_____ line 21

5. How much money did the woman give to Della for her hair?

The woman _____

_____ line 23

6. Della found the perfect gift for Jim. What was the gift?

_It_ _____

_____ line 27

Exercise C

Changing adjectives to adverbs. Many adverbs end in *ly*. You can make an adverb by adding *ly* to the end of an adjective. Study the chart.

Adjective	Adverb
slow	slow**ly**
quick	quick**ly**

An adverb usually tells something about a verb.

      verb   adverb

Della cried *softly*.

Complete the sentences with adverbs. The first one has been done for you.

1. Della counted the money <u>in a careful way</u>.

   Della counted the money ___*carefully*___.

2. Della cried <u>in a quiet way</u>.

   Della cried _____.

3. Della moved from the window <u>in a sudden way</u>.

   Della moved from the window _____.

4. She pulled down her hair <u>in a rapid way</u>.

   She pulled down her hair _____.

5. The time at the stores passed <u>in a quick way</u>.

   The time at the stores passed _____.

6. She looked at the gift, and her eyes shone <u>in a bright way</u>.

   She looked at the gift, and her eyes shone _____.

Exercise D

Understanding phrasal verbs. A phrasal verb is made up of a verb plus a preposition. The two words make a phrase.

Study the verb phrases at the left. Match them with their meanings. Write the correct letter in the blank. The first one has been done for you.

1. turned away ___*b*___
2. look for _____
3. look at _____
4. put on _____
5. pay for _____
6. went before _____

   a. add a piece of clothing
   b. stopped looking at
   c. try to find
   d. give money for
   e. stood in front of
   f. see; stare at

Exercise E

Using phrasal verbs. Complete the sentences with the phrasal verbs from Exercise D. Use each phrasal verb once. The first one has been done for you.

1. She needed money to ___*pay for*___ a gift.
2. Della suddenly decided to go out, so she hurried to _____ her jacket.
3. Della _____ the mirror. She wanted to see her hair.
4. Della didn't want to see her hair anymore. She _____ from the mirror.
5. The woman in the shop wanted to _____ Della's hair.
6. That afternoon Della went to _____ a special gift.

Exercise F

Understanding vocabulary. Read the words in the box. Write the words in the correct place in the chart. Some are done for you.

cent chops coffee couch dollar hat jacket mirror pay stairs stove window

Clothing	Food	Words about money	Things in a house
hat	chops	cent	mirror

Exercise G

Understanding vocabulary. Complete the crossword puzzle. Look at each clue. Find the correct word in the box. Write the word in the puzzle. One word has been done for you.

carpet   hurry   material   rare   fix   still   solid   worn

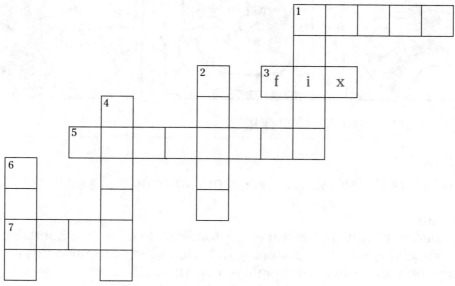

Across
1. strong and without errors
3. make better
5. what something is made of
7. not common or usual

Down
1. not moving
2. move quickly
4. something that covers a floor
6. old and used for a long time

Exercise H

Speaking up. Look at the conversation. Practice it with a partner.

SHARING WITH OTHERS

Activity A

Retelling the story. Retell the story. Imagine that you are Della.

Example:
I needed to buy a Christmas gift for Jim. He is my husband. He is special. I wanted a special gift. I tried to save money, but I had only one dollar and eighty-seven cents. . . .

Activity B

Sharing ideas. Everyone can learn by sharing ideas.
Discuss these questions with your partner or with the group.
Look up words you don't know. On a piece of paper, write your answer to one of the questions.

- What kind of person is Della?
  nice   nervous   loving   caring   stupid   thoughtful

- What problem did Della have?
  How did she solve it?
  Do you think it was a good solution? Why or why not?

Activity C

Guessing the ending. What do you think is going to happen? Will Jim like his gift? What will he think of Della's hair? Write down two ideas. Then share your ideas with the group.

THE GIFT OF THE MAGI

PART TWO

In part one of this story, Della had her hair cut off. Then she sold the hair. She bought her husband, Jim, a watch chain.

How do you think Jim will feel when he sees Della's hair?

Will he be happy with his gift?

The Gift of the Magi

based on a story by O. Henry

The door opened, and Jim walked in. He looked very **serious.**
Poor fellow, he was only twenty-two. He needed a new overcoat,
and he was without gloves.

Immediately his eyes fixed on Della. She didn't understand their
expression: It was not anger or surprise. He simply stared at her.

"Jim, darling," she **cried,** "don't look at me that way. I had my
hair cut off, and I sold it. I wanted to give you a present. You
don't mind, do you? My hair grows fast. Say 'Merry Christmas!' "

"You cut off your hair?" asked Jim, slowly.

"Yes," said Della. "Don't you like me just as well? I'm still me
without my hair."

"Your hair is gone?" he asked again. He didn't seem to believe it.

"It's sold," said Della. "Should I put the chops on, Jim?"

Suddenly Jim hugged Della. He took a package from his pocket.
"A haircut can't change my feelings for you, Dell," he said. "Open
this package. You'll see why I stared."

Her fingers tore at the paper. There was a scream of joy—and
then tears.

There in Della's hands were The Combs. Della had seen these
combs in the window of a **fancy** store. She had wanted them so
very much. They were beautiful combs with **jewels** on their
edges. Now they were hers—but most of her hair was gone. Now
her hair was too short for the combs!

Finally Della said, "My hair grows so fast, Jim!" Suddenly she
jumped up. She had forgotten about Jim's present. She held the
watch chain out to him and smiled. "I **looked all over** town for a
special gift for you. You'll have to look at the time a hundred
times a day from now on. Give me your watch."

Jim smiled. He said, "Let's put our presents away. They're too
nice to use right now. I sold the watch. I used the money to buy
your combs. Now why don't you put the chops on?"

****

The Magi were wise men from Asia. Long ago they **invented** the
art of giving Christmas presents. Their gifts were no doubt good.

You have just read the tale of two foolish young people. They
each **gave up** their greatest treasure. They each wanted to give
the other a special gift. But some may say that these two were
the wisest of all givers of gifts.

YOU CAN ANSWER THESE QUESTIONS

Put an *x* in the box next to the correct answer.

Reading Comprehension

1. When Jim first looked at Della, he was
- ❏ a. upset.
- ❏ b. not angry.

2. Della looked different because
- ❏ a. her hair was short.
- ❏ b. her clothes were new.

3. Jim gave Della
- ❏ a. a necklace.
- ❏ b. combs for her hair.

4. Della could not use the combs because
- ❏ a. her hair was too short.
- ❏ b. she didn't like them.

5. Jim could not use the watch chain because he had
- ❏ a. lost his watch.
- ❏ b. sold his watch.

6. Jim and Della were foolish because they
- ❏ a. had no money.
- ❏ b. were not able to use their gifts.

7. Jim and Della were wise because they
- ❏ a. showed their love for each other.
- ❏ b. learned not to buy expensive gifts.

Vocabulary

8. Jim looked serious. The word *serious* means
- ❏ a. tired and old.
- ❏ b. not laughing or having fun.

Idioms

9. Della asked Jim, "You don't mind, do you?" The idiom *don't mind* means
- ❏ a. aren't happy about.
- ❏ b. aren't angry or feeling bad about.

10. Della looked all over for the watch chain. The idiom *looked all over* means
- ❏ a. looked down from a high place.
- ❏ b. looked everywhere.

How many questions did you answer correctly? Circle your score. Then fill in your score on the Score Chart on page 153.

Number Correct	1	2	3	4	5	6	7	8	9	10
Score	10	20	30	40	50	60	70	80	90	100

Exercise A

Building sentences. Make sentences by adding the correct letter. The first one has been done for you.

1. The door opened, and ___*b*___

2. Jim didn't seem to _____

3. Jim gave _____

4. Della opened the package and _____

    a. Della a package.
    b. Jim walked in.
    c. believe that Della's hair was short.
    d. started to cry.

Now write the sentences on the lines below. Begin each sentence with a capital letter. End it with a period.

1. _____

2. _____

3. _____

4. _____

Now do numbers 5–8 the same way.

5. Inside the package were _____

6. Della's hair was _____

7. Della gave the watch chain _____

8. Jim didn't _____

    a. combs.
    b. to Jim.
    c. too short for the combs.
    d. have his watch.

5. _____

6. _____

7. _____

8. _____

Exercise B

Understanding the story. Answer each question in a complete sentence. Look back at the line numbers in the story. End each sentence with a period. The first one has been done for you.

1. Who came into the apartment?

   Jim came into the apartment.

   _____

2. What person did he look at?

   He looked at _____

   _____ line 4

3. What did Jim give Della?

   He gave her _____

   _____ line 19

4. Why did Della cry?

   She cried because her hair _____

   _____ line 23

5. What did Jim sell?

   Jim sold _____

   _____ line 30

6. What did Jim want to do with the gifts?

   Jim _____

   _____ line 29

Exercise C

Using the past tense. Retell the whole story. Write complete sentences. Use the past-tense forms of the verbs. Some verbs are regular, and some are irregular.

1. Della / count her money

   Della counted her money.

2. She / have a problem

3. She / need money for a gift for her husband

4. She / go to a shop

5. She / sell her hair

6. She / get her husband a watch chain

7. Jim / come home

8. He / look at Della's hair for a long time

9. He / give her some combs

10. Della / hold out the watch chain

11. They / put away their gifts

Exercise D

Using the infinitive form to tell why. In English the infinitive has the form *to* + verb. Infinitives are sometimes used to tell why. Study the chart.

Why question	infinitive
Why did Della go to the mirror?	*to look*
Sentence with infinitive to tell why:	
Della went to the mirror *to look* at her hair.	

Match the questions with the answers. The answer is an infinitive plus some other words. Use the information from both parts of the story to find the answers. The first one has been done for you.

_c_ **1.** Why did Della want to sell her hair?	**a.** *to fix* her hair
____ **2.** Why did Della go to the first shop?	**b.** *to look* for a present for her husband
____ **3.** Why did Della go to the stores?	**c.** *to get* money for a gift for her husband
____ **4.** Why did Della use curling irons?	**d.** *to get* money for a gift for his wife
____ **5.** Why did Jim sell his watch?	**e.** *to sell* her hair
____ **6.** Why did Jim want money?	**f.** *to buy* combs for his wife

Exercise E

Using the infinitive form to tell why. Complete the sentences to answer the questions in Exercise D. Use infinitives. The first one has been done for you.

1. _Della wanted to get money for a gift for her husband._

2. _Della went_ _____

3. _Della went_ _____

4. _Della_ _____

5. _Jim_ _____

6. _Jim_ _____

Exercise F
Using prepositions. Complete the sentences with the prepositions in the box. Use each preposition once. The first one has been done for you.

at	for	from	in	of	to	without

1. Jim was poor. He was _without_ gloves.

2. He looked _____ Della for a long time.

3. He took a package _____ his pocket.

4. He gave the gift _____ Della.

5. He saw the combs _____ the window _____ a store.

6. Della said, "I have a gift _____ you."

Exercise G
Adding vocabulary. On the left are words from the story. Complete each sentence by adding the correct word. Put the correct letter of the sentence next to the word. The first one has been done for you.

_b_ **1.** cried

_____ **2.** immediately

_____ **3.** invented

_____ **4.** jewels

_____ **5.** fancy

_____ **6.** expression

a. When Jim walked in, his eyes _____ fixed on Della. He looked at her right away

b. "Jim, darling," Della _____ when her husband stared at her. She said it loudly.

c. The combs had _____ in them. They shone in the light.

d. Della didn't understand the _____ in Jim's eyes. She couldn't tell what he was thinking.

e. The Magi _____ the art of giving Christmas gifts. The Magi were the first people to give them.

f. The combs were in a _____ store. The store had many beautiful and expensive things.

Exercise H
Speaking up. Look at the conversation. Practice it with a partner.

Sharing with others

Activity A

Readers Theater. Do this activity in groups.

1. Practice reading the story. Imagine you are preparing a radio play. Assign two readers to be narrators. Other readers should take the roles of Della, Jim, and Madame Sofronie.

2. Have groups share their radio plays.

Activity B

Sharing ideas. Everyone can learn by sharing ideas. Discuss these questions with your partner or with the group. Write your answer to one of the questions.

• Was the ending a surprise to you? Why or why not?
  Look back at page 120. You wrote your idea for the ending.
  How close was your idea to the real ending?

• What problem did the couple have at the end?
  What was the problem with the two presents?

• Do you think that the ending was happy or sad? Why?

• Do you think that Jim and Della were foolish? Why or why not?
  Do you think that Jim and Della were wise? Why or why not?

• What was your favorite part of the story? Read it to a partner.

THE SOW, THE MARE, AND THE COW

PART ONE

Think about what the word *home* means to you.

What do you like about your home? What would you change about it?

If you could choose any place, where would you like to live?

The Sow, the Mare, and the Cow

by Jane Yolen

Not so very long ago, a sow, a mare, and a cow were friends. They lived together on a farm in a green and pleasant land.

One day the sow said to her friends, "I **am tired of** man and his fences. I want to see the world." She grunted this so loudly that all the other animals on the farm heard her and turned their backs. But her friends did not. "I agree," said the mare. "And I," said the cow.

So that very night, the cow and the mare **leaped** over the fence; the sow crawled under. Then the three companions went one hoof after another down the road to see the world. But the world was full of men and fences all down the road.

The sow shook her head. "I am going into the **woods,**" she said. "I agree," said the mare. "And I," said the cow. So they pushed through branch after branch, and bramble after briar, till the way grew dark and tangled. At last they found a small **clearing** where no fence had ever been built and no man had ever dwelt. They settled there for the night.

The sow and the mare took turns **standing guard**, but the cow fell right to sleep. The mare began to **nod.** Then the sow. Soon all three were asleep, and no one was left to guard the others in the small clearing in the dark wood. Suddenly a low growling filled the forest.

The sow and the mare woke up **with a start.** The cow lowed in alarm and hid her eyes with her hooves. The growling got louder. The cow jumped up. Back to back, the three friends spent the rest of the night awake and **trembling.**

25 In the morning the sow said, "I think we should build a barn. Then we will be safe from the growlers in the night." "I agree," said the mare. "And I," said the cow.

So the mare gathered twigs and **boughs** for walls. The sow rooted leaves and moss for the **roof.** And the cow showed them
30 where everything should be placed.

Branch by branch, bramble after briar, they built a fine barn.

That night the three friends went inside their barn. The sow and mare took turns standing guard, but the cow fell right to sleep. The mare began to nod. Then the sow.

35 Soon all three were asleep, and no one was left to guard the others in the fine barn in the small clearing in the dark wood. Suddenly a high howling filled the forest.

The sow and the mare woke up with a start. The cow lowed in alarm and tried to hide in a corner. The howling got higher and
40 closer.

YOU CAN ANSWER THESE QUESTIONS

Put an *x* in the box next to the correct answer.

Reading Comprehension

1. In the beginning, the three animals lived
   - ❏ a. on the same farm.
   - ❏ b. on different farms.

2. The sow was tired of
   - ❏ a. man and his fences.
   - ❏ b. farmwork.

3. When the sow first talked about her plan,
   - ❏ a. all of the animals wanted to go with her.
   - ❏ b. the mare and the cow agreed to go with her.

4. All down the road the three animals saw
   - ❏ a. no men and fences.
   - ❏ b. many men and fences.

5. The three animals went into
   - ❏ a. a field.
   - ❏ b. the woods.

6. On the first night in the forest, the three animals heard a growling sound, and they
   - ❏ a. were afraid.
   - ❏ b. ran away.

7. On the second day in the forest, the three animals built
   - ❏ a. a barn.
   - ❏ b. a fence.

Vocabulary

8. The animals went into the woods. The word *woods* means
   - ❏ a. tree branches.
   - ❏ b. forest.

Idioms

9. One animal was standing guard at night. The idiom *standing guard* means
   - ❏ a. watching over others.
   - ❏ b. standing beside someone.

10. The sound surprised them, and the sow and the mare woke up with a start. The idiom *with a start* means
    - ❏ a. with a sudden action.
    - ❏ b. very slowly and carefully.

How many questions did you answer correctly? Circle your score. Then fill in your score on the Score Chart on page 153.

Number Correct	1	2	3	4	5	6	7	8	9	10
Score	10	20	30	40	50	60	70	80	90	100

EXERCISES TO HELP YOU

Exercise A

Building sentences. Make sentences by adding the correct letter. The first one has been done for you.

1. A sow, a mare, and a cow ___*d*___

    a. to see the world.
    b. go with her.
    c. full of men and fences.
    d. lived together on a farm.

2. The sow wanted _____

3. Her friends agreed to _____

4. At first, the world was _____

Now write the sentences on the lines below. Begin each sentence with a capital letter. End it with a period.

1. _____

2. _____

3. _____

4. _____

Now do numbers 5–8 the same way.

5. The three animals _____

    a. a low growling.
    b. trembling the rest of the night.
    c. were in the woods.
    d. build a barn.

6. The animals heard _____

7. They were _____

8. The sow thought that they should _____

5. _____

6. _____

7. _____

8. _____

Exercise B

Understanding the story. Answer each question in a complete sentence. Look back at the line numbers in the story. End each sentence with a period. The first one has been done for you.

1. Where did the animals live at first?

They lived on a farm.

2. What was the sow tired of?

She was tired of

_____ lines 3–4

3. Who agreed to go with the sow to see the world?

and   _agreed to go_

with the sow.   line 4

4. Where did the animals settle?

They settled in a small

_____ lines 14–16

5. What did they hear the first night?

They heard a

_____ line 20

6. What did they build?

_____ line 25

Exercise C

Using *should* for advice and to make suggestions. The word *should* is often used when giving advice. It is also used when making suggestions about what to do. Study the chart.

***Should* for advice and suggestions**
should + verb
We *should build* a barn.
Someone *should stay* awake.

Complete the sentences with *should* and the verb under the line. The first one has been done for you.

1. The sow thought, "I ___*should see*___ the world."

see

2. In the woods, the sow thought, "Someone
   _____ the others."

guard

3. The cow _____ awake.

stay

4. The three animals _____ who is making the sounds.

learn

Write sentences about friendship. Give advice and use the word *should.* An example has been done for you.

5. *A friend should help a friend.*

6. _____

7. _____

Exercise D

Understanding adjectives + *of*. Some adjectives are followed by the preposition *of*. Study the chart.

afraid of   full of   tired of
Example: The sow was *tired of* fences.

Complete the sentences with adjectives and prepositions from the chart. The first one is done for you.

1. The world outside the farm was ___*full of*___ men and fences.

2. The sow was _____ men.

3. The woods were _____ trees.

4. The three animals were _____ the strange noises in the night. They trembled.

Exercise E

Understanding vocabulary. Match the verbs from the story with their meanings. Write the correct letter in the blank.

1. crawled _____
2. settled _____
3. leaped _____
4. nod _____
5. tremble _____

   a. made a home
   b. jumped
   c. shake, often because of something scary
   d. moved by using arms and legs while close to the ground
   e. move the head up and down

Exercise F

Using vocabulary. Complete the sentences. Use the verbs in Exercise E.

1. The animals left the farm. The mare _____ over the fence.

2. The sow _____ under the fence.

3. The animals pushed through the woods. They _____ in a clearing.

4. The sow and mare started to _____. They both were soon asleep.

5. The three animals heard a low growling. They started to _____.

Exercise G

Understanding vocabulary. Answer the riddles. Use the words in the box. Write the correct answer in the blank. The first one has been done for you.

barn	bough	fence	hoof	mare	roof

1. I am a female horse.

   What am I? ___mare___

2. I am the name for the foot of horses, cows, and other animals.

   What am I? _____

3. I am part of a tree.

   What am I? _____

4. I am a place for animals, such as horses and cows.

   What am I? _____

5. I go around places. I protect things inside me.

   What am I? _____

6. I am the top part of a house. I cover it.

   What am I? _____

Speaking up. Look at the conversation. Practice it with a partner.

SHARING WITH OTHERS

Activity A

Retelling the story. Imagine that you are the sow, the mare, or the cow. Tell a classmate the story in your own words.

Example
The mare: I lived on a farm in a green and pleasant land. My friend the sow had an idea. She wanted to see the world. She didn't want to live near man and his fences. I said, "I agree."

Activity B

Sharing ideas. Everyone can learn by sharing ideas. Discuss these questions with your partner or with the group.

• Which of the following phrases are about the sow? Which are about the mare? Which are about the cow? Some phrases may be about more than one animal. Give reasons for your answers.

has new ideas
is willing to try new things
is a leader
is sometimes afraid
is willing to help friends
wants to be free and away from man
lets others make decisions

Then discuss the following questions.

What do you think is going to happen?
What is making the scary sounds?

THE SOW, THE MARE, AND THE COW

PART TWO

This is part two of the fable. At the end of part one, the animals were in the woods. They were scared.
Where do you think the animals will be at the end of the story?

Think about how each animal behaved in part one.
Do you think the animals did the right thing when they moved from the farm to the woods?

The Sow, the Mare, and the Cow

by Jane Yolen

The sow ran to guard the door. The mare ran to guard the window. The cow turned her face to the wall. The three friends spent the rest of the night awake and trembling.

In the morning, the sow said, "I think we should build a high fence around our fine barn to **keep away** the growlers and the howlers in the night." "I agree," said the mare. "And I," said the cow. So the mare gathered logs and **stumps.** The sow pushed **boulders** and stones. And the cow showed them where everything should be placed.

Then stick by stone, and bramble after briar, they built themselves a high fence. The three friends went inside their fine barn, which was inside their high fence, to spend the night. The sow and mare took turns standing guard, but the cow fell right to sleep. The mare began to nod. Then the sow. Soon all three were asleep, and no one was left to guard the others in the fine barn inside the high fence in the small clearing in the dark wood.

Suddenly there was a **scratching** at the door and a scrambling on the roof. The sow and mare awoke with a start. The cow lowed in alarm and fell to her knees. They waited for someone or something to enter. But nothing did.

Still the three friends spent the rest of the night awake and trembling. In the morning the three friends were tired and **pale** and a little uncertain. They looked at one another and at the fine barn inside the high fence in the small clearing in the dark wood.

25 Then the cow spoke. "I have a sudden great **longing** for man and his fences." But the mare did not say, "I agree." And the sow did not say, "And I." They were suddenly both too busy digging ditches, fixing fences, **mending** roofs, and laying a path to their door.

So the cow put one hoof after another **all the way back** to the
30 farm in the middle of the green and pleasant land. There she lived a long and happy life **within** man's fences.

But the sow and the mare opened the door that very night and met the growlers and the howlers, the scratchers and the scrabblers who were just the forest folk who had come to **make**
35 **them welcome.**

And they too lived long and happy lives within fences of their own making. And if you can tell which one of the three was the happiest, you are a better judge of animals than I.

YOU CAN ANSWER THESE QUESTIONS

Put an *x* in the box next to the correct answer.

Reading Comprehension

1. On the third night, the animals
   - ❏ a. didn't hear any strange sounds.
   - ❏ b. heard sounds, but nothing entered the barn.

2. On the third morning, the cow said that she wanted to
   - ❏ a. see man and his fences again.
   - ❏ b. build another fence.

3. The sow and the mare
   - ❏ a. asked the cow to stay.
   - ❏ b. did much work.

4. The cow had
   - ❏ a. a happy life on the farm.
   - ❏ b. problems on the farm without her friends.

5. The sounds at night were from
   - ❏ a. dangerous animals.
   - ❏ b. friendly animals.

6. The sow and the mare had
   - ❏ a. a happy life on their own land.
   - ❏ b. a nice barn but no fence.

7. The cow was happy
   - ❏ a. living within man's fences.
   - ❏ b. living within her own fences.

Vocabulary

8. The sow and the mare worked to mend the roof. The word *mend* means
   - ❏ a. build something.
   - ❏ b. fix something.

9. The cow had a longing for her farm. *Longing* means
   - ❏ a. a strong need.
   - ❏ b. a long wait.

Idioms

10. The three animals wanted to keep away the growlers and the howlers. *Keep away* means
    - ❏ a. scare with noise.
    - ❏ b. stop from getting close.

How many questions did you answer correctly? Circle your score. Then fill in your score on the Score Chart on page 153.

Number Correct	1	2	3	4	5	6	7	8	9	10
Score	10	20	30	40	50	60	70	80	90	100

EXERCISES TO HELP YOU

Exercise A

Building sentences. Make sentences by adding the correct letter. The first one has been done for you.

1. The animals were _____*a*_____
2. They built a _____
3. On the third night, _____
4. Nothing entered _____

   a. afraid the second night.
   b. the barn.
   c. fence around their barn.
   d. they heard noises at the door and on the roof.

Now write the sentences on the lines below. Begin each sentence with a capital letter. End it with a period.

1. _____

2. _____

3. _____

   _____

4. _____

Do numbers 5–8 the same way.

5. On the third morning, the animals _____
6. The cow said that she wanted to _____
7. The sounds were _____
8. All three animals lived _____

   a. go back to the farm.
   b. from animals in the forest.
   c. were tired and pale.
   d. long and happy lives.

5. _____

6. _____

7. _____

8. _____

Exercise B

Understanding the story. Answer each question in a complete sentence. Look back at the line numbers in the story. End each sentence with a period. The first one has been done for you.

1. What did the sow want to build next?

   She wanted to build a high fence.

   _____

2. What did the three animals hear at the door on the third night?

   They heard a _____

   _____ line 17

3. How did they feel the next morning?

   They were _____

   _____ lines 22–23

4. Where did the cow want to go?

   She wanted to go back to _____

   _____ line 30

5. Where did the cow live at the end?

   She lived within _____

   _____ line 31

6. Where did the sow and the mare live at the end?

   _____

   _____ lines 36–37

Exercise C

Using question words. To ask questions, you can use the words *who, what, when, where,* and *why.* Study this chart.

Who	for people	Who had farms and fences? *Men* had farms and fences.
What	for things	What did the animals build? They built a *barn* and a *fence.*
When	for time	When did they hear noises? They heard noises *at night.*
Where	for places	Where did the animals sleep? They slept *in the barn.*
Why	for reasons	Why did the cow leave? The cow left *because she was afraid.*

Complete each question with the correct question word. Use the answer for clues. The first one has been done for you.

1. _*What*_____ did the sow run to guard?

The sow ran to guard **the door.**

2. _____ did the animals build next?

The animals built **a high fence** next.

3. _____ were the animals afraid during the night?

They were afraid during the night **because they heard strange sounds.**

4. _____ did they build a high fence?

They built a high fence **around the barn.**

5. _____ did the cow leave the forest?

The cow left the forest **on the third morning.**

6. _____ lived happy lives?

The sow, the mare, and the cow lived happy lives.

Exercise D

Making questions. Write questions for the answers. Follow the directions. Some have been done for you.

Make questions that start with the word *who*.

1. *Who lived on a farm?*

A sow, a mare, and a cow lived on a farm.

2. _____

The sow wanted to see the world.

Make questions that start with the word *where*.

3. *Where did the sow, the mare, and the cow go?*

The sow, the mare, and the cow went **to the woods.**

4. _____

The cow went **back to the farm.**

5. _____

The sow and the mare stayed **in the forest.**

Make questions that start with the word *when*.

6. *When did the animals leave the farm?*

The animals left the farm **at night.**

7. _____

The animals built a barn **on their first day in the woods.**

8. _____

The sow and the mare opened their door **one night.**

Exercise E

Adding an adjective. Complete the sentences by adding the correct adjective. Use each adjective once. Write the letter of the sentence next to the adjective that goes with the sentence. The first one has been done for you.

1. awake __*a*__	a. The animals were _____ after they heard strange sounds.
2. busy _____	b. The sow wanted to build a _____ fence. She wanted to keep away the animals that made the noises.
3. green and pleasant _____	c. The animals didn't sleep much and they were afraid. So they were all _____ the next morning.
4. high _____	d. The cow left, but the sow and the mare were _____ with their work.
5. long and happy _____	e. The cow went back to the _____ land.
6. tired and pale _____	f. All three animals had _____ lives after the cow left.

Exercise F

Understanding vocabulary. Match each word below with its meaning. Next to the word, write the letter of the meaning.

1. stump _____

2. boulder _____

3. scratching _____

4. ditch _____

5. log _____

a. a sound made with fingernails or claws

b. a long, thin hole in the ground

c. what is left of a tree after it has been cut down

d. a thick piece of wood from the main part of a tree

e. a large rock

Exercise G

Speaking up. Look at the conversation. Practice it with a partner.

SHARING WITH OTHERS

Activity A

Acting out the fable. Work in groups of five or six.

1. Make masks for the characters in the story: the cow, the sow, the mare, and other animals. You might also make masks to show the animals' faces.
2. One or two people can read the story. The others can use the masks and act as the animals.
3. Groups can take turns acting out the fable.

Activity B

Sharing ideas. Everyone can learn by sharing ideas. Discuss these questions with your partner or with the group. Write your answers to one of the questions.

• In your own words, tell the lesson of the story.
• How would you describe the two kinds of life in the story? You can use the list below for help.

> making your own decisions
> following other people's decisions
> being safe
> having freedom
> being afraid of new things
> liking new things

• Who do you think made the right choice—the cow, or the sow and the mare?
  Which life would you like more?

SCORE CHART

This is the Score Chart for You Can Answer These Questions.
Shade in your score for each unit. For example, if your score
was 80 for **Why the Monsoon Comes Every Year,** look at the
bottom of the chart for **Why the Monsoon Comes Every Year.**
Shade in the bar up to the 80 mark. By looking at this chart,
you can see how well you did on each unit.

Score	100								100
	90								90
	80								80
	70								70
	60								60
	50								50
	40								40
	30								30
	20								20
	10								10
Story Title	Why the Monsoon Comes Every Year	A Lesson from Two Little Girls	How the People Became Wise	The Envelope	The Smell of Food and the Sound of Coins	Don Quixote and the Windmills	Beginnings	The Farmer and the Circus	

	Perseus	Apples, Apples	The Neglected Grandfather	The Gift of the Magi: Part One	The Gift of the Magi: Part Two	The Sow, the Mare, and the Cow: Part One	The Sow, the Mare, and the Cow: Part Two	
100								100
90								90
80								80
70								70
60								60
50								50
40								40
30								30
20								20
10								10